Body Language

The Guide to How to Recognize the Hidden Meaning Behind People's Gestures and Expressions

Kate Cooper

Contents

INTRODUCTION

- Do you want to explore most powerful behaviors that reveal our confidence and true sentiments?
- Do you want to learn to know how does body language work?

Much investigation and exchange exist to determine whether non-verbal signs are natural, learned, hereditarily moved, or non-inheritable. The examination is ordered from the perception of the visually impaired and hard of hearing - those that couldn't have learned non-verbal signs through the conventional sociological sound or visual stations, from the investigation of the gestural conduct of the fluctuated societies throughout the planet and examination concerning the lead of our closest sociology family members, the chimps, and monkeys. The German Eibl-Eibesfeldt tracked down that young people's grinning articulations conceived as hard of hearing and visually impaired happen while not typical sociological molding. It proposes that these could even be inherent motions. Ekman, Friesen, and Sorenson upheld Darwin's essential convictions regarding periodic signals once they contemplated individuals' outward appearances from 5 inside and out completely various societies. Astonished, they tracked down that each culture utilized indistinguishable fundamental facial motions to call attention to the feeling. It drove them to the end that these signals ought to be inherent. When you fold your arms on your chest, are your arm gotten left over right or directly over left? The overall population can't with certainty portray that approach; they follow common natural sense.

The discussion exists on whether a few signals are socially educated and get routine or innately hereditary. For example, most men put on a coat right arm introductory while most young ladies place it on the left arm first, which shows the contrast between every sexual orientation. When somebody passes a lady on a congested road, he once in a while turns his body towards her as he passes; she in some cases diverts her body standoffish from him. Does she intuitively endeavor this to protect her bosoms? Is this a partner's innate ladylike response, or has she figured out how to function to the present by unwittingly needing elective females? A large portion of our important non-verbal conduct is learned, and this conjointly implies that a huge load of our developments and motions are socially decided. It gives us the benefit of testing these parts of visual correspondence in a few societies and social orders. A large portion of the fundamental correspondence signals is indistinguishable wherever the globe. When people are upbeat, they grin; when they're sad or angry, they grimace or glower. Gesturing the head is generally acquainted with point 'yes' or confirmation. It appears to be a vogue of head bringing down related as a characteristic motion since hard of hearing and visually impaired people also use it. Shaking the head from one highlight to another specifies 'no' or invalidation and is also all-inclusive and ought to be fairly a signal learned in the earliest stages.

When a child has had sufficient milk, he diverts his head from one highlight to another to dismiss his mom's bosom. When the little youngster has had enough to eat, he shakes his head from highlight reason to stop his parent's set up to satisfy him. During this methodology, he rapidly figures out how to utilize the apex shaking motion to reason out conflict or a negative perspective. One in everything about the most powerful correspondence methods we tend to use in our everyday connections is our non-verbal or body language. It is the method of correspondence that touches off our "gut-level" feelings and reactions. The examination has shown that getting a comprehension of body language builds one's capacity to acquire something one asks for in unexpected situations. Have you at any point watched a couple sitting along and in minutes knew how great or unfortunate their relationship was? Did you at any point can't help thinking about how you were prepared to return to this end subsequently rapidly with no immediate connection? Regardless of whether you're aware of it or not, we will, in general, compensate our days reacting to individuals' non-verbal signs projected through their body language and making inferences about them from our perceptions. Our body language uncovers the truth we stow away with our words from the world, including how we tend to feel about ourselves, our connections, and our things. Through our eye-to-eye connection, signals, body position, and outward appearances, the people we tend to interface with will confirm our aims, the nature of our connections, how breathtaking we tend to are in some random situation, our certainty level, and what our true inspirations and requirements are.

The force of body language is found inside the passionate reaction it makes. Sentiments drive choices and responses in pretty much every situation. Non-verbal signals trigger emotions that decide an individual's center resources like honesty, reliability, genuineness, expertise level, and initiative capacities. Understanding these signals will confirm who we tend to date, the obligation we get utilized for, what level of progress we tend to get, and even who could be chosen into influential political positions. With a particularly fundamental ability, why don't we tend to pay years learning and creating successful body language abilities? The fact of the matter is most people underestimate the significance of body language until they are searching for a more profound comprehension of human conduct in an exceptionally close-to-home relationship or to accomplish a grasp in a serious business situation. Authority of body language gives people the keys to decipher what implies behind clear signals and body development, giving a comprehension on an approach to project and conveying messages successfully while overseeing others. Thereupon, generally, the viability of relational connections is incredibly expanded.

The best way to deal with a start this technique for dominance is to get familiar with the fundamental translation of the two center body language sorts - open presence and shut presence. The shut presence body language sort is highlighted in individuals who crease their body round the body's middle line, which runs straight down the center of the body from the high of the head to the feet. The essential qualities that produce this sort of essence are feet put near one another, arms held shut to the body, hands crossed on the body or held together before the body, little hand signals held shut to the body, shoulders moved forward, and eyes focused underneath eye level. The messages conveyed to the globe by the shut presence of body language are uncertainty, low vanity, frailty, and an absence of skill. In outrageous cases, one will even create the message of urgency to be imperceptible. The consequences for the individual extending such a body language can differ from just not getting the best chances feasible to the direst outcome imaginable of holding an inevitable read of exploitation.

In differentiation, the open presence is included in individuals who make a feeling of power, force, and authority by projecting certainty, achievement, strength, and ability dominance. The actual attributes are feet held hip wide separated, open hand signals utilized in discussion a long way from focus line of the body, elbows held detached from the body, shoulders kept down, straight positions, and eyes focused at the eye level of their audience members. These individuals are viewed as appealing, fruitful, intelligent, and appear to have achievement come just. We will, in general, view this body language type because of the "body language of pioneers." To improve body language and begin to project an open presence, the key is eye to eye connection. Eye to eye connection is one of the most vital specialized apparatuses we own. By utilizing direct eye to eye connection while communicating with others, one can change how individuals see them.

When individuals start to talk straightforwardly at someone, they're viewed as guaranteed, reliable, and gifted. Hand motions and facial demeanor are the second degrees of alteration one can make to be seen with open presence. These methods of correspondence loan themselves to expanding the capacity to impart messages unmistakably and successfully. By utilizing open hand signals from the body and expressive facial affect handily, a more prominent effect is framed when talking by changing into all the more outwardly animating to the audience and expanding the amount of data given during the association. As adolescents, since the beginning, we tend to are encouraged that intelligent young men and ladies sit appropriately with legs together and hands collapsed before them. The consolation to restrict actual region as children will make some of the attributes found in the body language of the shut presence in adulthood. To counter this outcome, one can start to embrace the qualities of the open presence of body language and join these habits into their normal condition. When this conduct adjustment is finished, it can offer the indistinguishable non-verbal impressions and messages as their open presence partners. The dominance of body language is imperative to making the best presence in every single relational connection. While not this dominance, individuals are in danger of being misjudged and notice their endeavors to convey their thoughts ineffective. With the ability to separate between the different body language methods, anybody will accomplish the dominance important to get fruitful in whichever try they select. If you understand it, body language might be a huge issue answerable for how everybody you meet arrives at an assessment concerning you. In a few callings, essentially in callings where you work with others, listening abilities are an unquestionable requirement and appallingly significant for making shrewd associations with customers.

Whether you help individuals keep up their connections, offering steerage to individuals for satisfaction in business, or direct people for some other sort of issue, they are seeing your body language, showing great listening abilities makes people extra comfortable. Helpless Body language could Result in you Losing out on something gigantic. It isn't critical to such an extent that you just! are tuning in to every single word cautiously and genuinely. Your body language produces others to feel significant which you are giving them the consideration they need. Here it's indispensable to comprehend the indications of a helpless audience, and you ought to endeavor to free yourself of any of these.

On the off chance that you are prone to keep your arms collapsed over your chest, else you tap your toes fretfully, lean or flip to appear to be away too commonly, or look to a great extent constantly while tuning in, at that point, you are telling the other individual who you're not intrigued by what the person is saying. It can bring about the tip of the association and can cause enormous misfortunes in business. Anyway, what will you are doing, with the goal that your body language begins to convey positive messages to the individual you're conversing with? Initially, it would help if you endeavored to confront the contrary individual sq. on.

Try not to turn away to convey a positive message. At that point, we tend to get back to the reason for your body at the hour of correspondence. It would help if you accepted an open stance. You need never keep your arms or legs collapsed, or the consequences will be severe. The other individual will expect that you're not interested in tuning in to their motivation. Assuming you fit forward while conversing with somebody, your body language says you're giving a ton of consideration to what the individual in question is saying. In differentiation, inclining away demonstrates that you have no revenue what subsequently ever. At that point, we get back to the consideration contact. Eye to eye connection is the chief vital issue. Consistently attempt to keep in touch typically. Assuming you hold attempting down or turning away, it shows that you're not showing any interest in the point and feeling awkward. Also, the significance of a casual stance can furthermore not be overlooked. Try not to attempt to be excessively solid.

Neither should you be excessively formal while conversing with somebody. If you feel that you have endured colossal misfortunes in the past because of your helpless body language, at that point, you should begin rehearsing the previously mentioned tips right away. Your body language starts talking for you the second you leave your home. In any event, when you're not talking, how you stand, how you sit, and how you use your hands, this is the thing that others comprehend as correspondence. Thus, if you don't have an unmistakable comprehension of body language, by and large, your body language will not match what your aims are, and people can get the wrong message. When your body language negates your aims, it might cause a huge misfortune for you since you will lose your validity. Like this, what should you be doing to keep up your validity? We tend to first gain proficiency with a next to no more about body language, be a ton of trustworthy and a ton of talented inside others' eyes. At whatever point you meet your customer for a business, make your passageway as sure as achievable. How might you do this? It would help if you began by discussing the business while you enter the premises of the customer. Poring over the papers or glancing through your attaché will send a bad introduction. Regardless of whether you need to go to some time, the best methodology is to look over any magazine.

Another fundamental tip identifying with body language is that you should shake hands heartily and immovably.

Then, we will, in general, go to the decision of seat to sit down on. You should never show that you will sit just when the other individual asks you to. All things being equal, you should choose the first worthy seat and sit right away. Be that as it may, never make the mistake of sitting excessively close or excessively route a long way from the customer. How much territory you should keep relies upon the character of the customer.

A back individual should take a seat at any distance than that of a friendly individual. Nonetheless, the ideal distance is between twenty to fifty inches. You will lean forward to ask closer to the client when endeavoring to put emphasize a specific point. Eye to eye connection is another fundamental portion of body language. Eye to eye connection and a grin on the face can send the message that you are a fair, genuine, and open individual. A dark eye to eye connection and attempting to a great extent now and again will send the message that you do not have sufficient trust in yourself. Likewise, keep away from consistently taking a gander at the contrary individual, as this will fabricate the client to feel very awkward. Ceaselessly endeavor to talk in your distinctive voice.

Chapter 1: What is Body Language & Its Importance

Body language is the language you express while not words. At the point when you say, "correspondence" you frequently consider "words," "addresses," and "introductions." Be that as it may, correspondence is significantly more than words. You can impart uncommonly precisely while not saying a single word only alongside your body. Every 50% of your body can talk as articulately as words; perhaps, significantly higher than words. The methods you stand, how you hold your head, the technique you position your palms, hands, arms, legs - everything says something. Now and then, you'll choose up the inferred message in a second - like when somebody is forceful - and in some cases, it requires some investment. Language is concerning correspondence. We will, in general, guess importance spoken; however, you might be stunned to discover that 90% of what we tend to speak with each other is implicit, as non-verbal 'signals' we will in general, offer each option through eye-to-eye connection, outward appearances, motions, stances and a determination of sounds and option tactile prompts. It is that the language of the body.

In general, we will utilize it repeatedly, various us a great deal of viably than others, and a ton of the time without acknowledging we are utilizing it. We tend to begin learning it in youth, essentially as we will figure out how to talk our primary language by picking up words and implications from our oldsters and everyone around us., the differentiation is that while botches in our communicated in language will, in general, be revised, they'll be missed, or confounded, in our body language - so you'll have the option to get more seasoned not understanding you're imparting seriously, or ineffectually. Subsequently, the clarification for this book. These signs and prompts send data about our thought processes, goals, and emotions. We utilize the body's language to pass on a wide range of messages and implications. The vast majority accept this cycle as a right, always failing to understand that it happens at a psyche instead of a conscious level. Essentially think concerning it briefly. Winks, squints, gestures, murmurs, and snorts - what number of those would you say you are truly aware of in the correspondence strategy? The intention is that language shouldn't be as words for your importance to be gotten a handle on by somebody else. The methods you utilize your body to underscore or suggest, tell, show, or maybe control resemble 'accentuation.' While not it, that implies and accentuation is lost. It would help if you exclusively considered the people, you most respect, or hatred, to see the significance of this body talk - the alluring ones who seem to attract people to them like magnets. Such magnets perpetually seem to encourage in your technique, those you envy who never seem to put a foot off-base, the peaceful ones whose eyes resemble swords. One thing in regards to their actual presence 'converses with' you.

Science Behind Body Language

Typically, the specific words we use to clarify conduct are reflected in our body language. For instance, cranky, people will, in general, show up 'down inside the mouth,' guaranteed people are supposed to be,' laid back,' self-assured people,' 'connect,' and along these lines forward. Since we tend tore not particularly savvy at perceiving the associations between body language and perspectives, we normally neglect to make the least complex o ourselves or the connections we tend to have with others. It's just when we look a great deal of intently that we will in general start to uncover things about and as well as other people that we've missed inside the course of our busy, regular day to day of the event that you don't think you are making the awesome yourself in close to home connections, at work, or just in your regular contact with individuals, the reasons, activities, and investigations toward the finish of each section should work with. You probably need to get a handle on an approach to turn into extra gifted in the use of body language and understand other people's utilization of it. A stack of examinations has been dispensed on non-verbal correspondence in the course of recent a very long time in shockingly named disciplines like paralinguistics, proxemics, chronemics, kinesics, and neurolinguistic programming. Be that as it may, distress over the expert terms, body language isn't advanced science. Improving your relational abilities might be a mix of sense, right perception, reflection, and application. It's somewhat similar to attempting at the celebs through a telescope, interestingly. Things you have missed with the unaided eye return strongly into the center - adding definition and that way to what you have everlastingly taken with no thought. "What does one peruse, my ruler?" "Words," said Hamlet. Methinks he should hath addressed "body language." Where a few groups are fixated on words, ceaselessly considering what we will, in general, will say straightaway, we give nearly almost no consideration to our body language. Odd just if 55% of correspondence is passed on through body language and just 7percent includes words. Take a moment to think about that fact. seven of correspondence is words. 57 is body language. It very well may be a stunning actuality, a reality that produces one thing clear: in case you're to take advantage of your relational abilities - social, proficient, or any place else- - you might want to frame utilization of body language. How, at that point, would you be able to spawn present resent time, to exploit that incredible, extraordinary 55p.c of correspondence that comes from body language? T

here are a decent a few different ways. How about we investigate a portion of the preeminent popular and generally crucial. Compromise: Perhaps you're one in every one of the disastrous individuals who seem to initiate in contentions commonly without a very great sign why. A few people appear to shape struggle apparently out of bounder. A bound person who will remain anonymous yet fills in as a magnificent model is now getting in contentions. He talks courteously. He never lets out the slightest peep off-base. In any case, he continues to get in contentions. Why? Since he has anxious body language. He creases his arms over his chest. He only very seldom grins. He'll tap on a table or other article while he talks. His words stay well mannered; in any case, his body language is not. His body language passes from bothered excessively forceful to anxious interminably.

On the off chance that your voice is loaded with energy, it will quickly get the client's eye. Your Tone of Voice is bountiful More Vital Than the specific Words You utilize Body language alludes to how you say your words instead of what you say. When you talk in your conventional tone and the volume is also in customary differ, at that point, your body language will be considered awesome. A very much adjusted voice with a typical beat and rate indicates demonstrable skill, showing revenue and energy. The sentences you utilize while talking ought to be just about as straightforward as feasible. On the contrary, hand, when you use "um" or "ah" or unnecessarily make a sound as if to speak, at that point, this sends a sign that you are feeling on edge. Assuming you might want to build up your body language, you should focus on your emotions and stances. Here are some straightforward suggestions on the most proficient method to upgrade pose. You ought to everlastingly stroll openly, making clear and decided strides with arms swinging yet should ascend in an erect stance. At the point when you keep an eye-to-eye connection with the contrary individual, cup your jaw between the thumb and in this manner the finger, or contact the scaffold of the nose with the hands or strike the jawline, at that point, you're showing that you are going to what in particular is being said.

A remarkable inverse, awful body language suggests apprehensive developments demonstrating the absence of consideration. In actuality, all you might want to do is try not to attempt on edge and keep yourself educated about the message you are communicating with body language. For instance, if you overlap your arms over your chest, fold your legs, endeavor to choose up build-up that is absent on your articles of clothing, or move your hands around all over, you're discussing your conflict with the point that the other individual is making. Flickering your eyes, again and again, hacking commonly, needing away at the hour of talking, and needing at better places by moving the eyes are demonstrative of negative viewpoint. If you reason your forefinger at something, you're showing your disappointment by your body language. Similarly, wringing your hands, getting a charge out of your hair, and holding your hands are pointers of your dissatisfaction. Presently, how can somebody exhibit that he is feeling exhausted? On the off chance that the eyes of the audience aren't focused on the person who is talking, on the off chance that he is sitting during a messy body pose, or if he is engrossed in doing one thing else as opposed to observing what is being said, at that point, he is showing that he's getting exhausted. The significance of body language will increment after you meet with people having a place with various societies.

Importance of Body Language
Body language is a part of communication that very few studies; however, it makes up most of what we will use to convey and is normally bountiful more right a pick, which implies the words we will utilize. I will share a few reasons why body language is essential and afterward offer you an extremely short test to decide how well you see it's that implies. They say talk is cheap, and for the most part, we will impart things even without the assistance of a solitary word. We will shrug our shoulders and, without a word, we have an inclination store said, "I don't have the foggiest idea." We will cause a stir, and we have a propensity stash essentially said, "Pardon me? Did I hear you right?" We can flip our hands over palms up in front of individuals to say, "I don't comprehend what else to refer to. That is all I have." In general, we will highlight our nose to the point that the contrary individual "has it right!" some of the things we will, in general, say with our bodies can work with us build up to why we tend to are saying it. Just saying "I don't get a handle on" has nothing on adding the accompanying motions. We tend to turn our hands over face up in front of individuals as we tend to cause a commotion and reverse our grin while we will, in general, stick our base lip somewhat out and appearance to the perspective. As of now, we've

additionally made somebody giggle and perhaps taken a touch of the crucial factor off ourselves, or the other individual who was somewhat anxious concerning not realizing regardless of it was we will, in general, didn't get a handle on.

Further, tuning in to somebody's body language will recognize when somebody isn't disclosing the full truth and nothing's reality. Here are a few signs that somebody may be lying. Frequently a one that isn't telling the truth or the entirety of the truth won't have any desire to frame eye to eye connection for concern the eyes are the windows to their lying spirits. In any case, there are additional elective indications of lying. An individual who isn't telling every bit of relevant information may make a sound as if to speak, stammer, or revision their pitch as though to endeavor and influence your consideration away from their falsehood or to slow down; hence they may have the opportunity to expect up an exact answer or conceivable explanation. Moreover, foot-tapping or ricocheting, becoming flushed, putting their hand to their face, dismissing or raising their shoulders may all be pointers that they're awkward with the discussion since they're not telling the truth. Another vital work of body language is too explicit our sentiments concerning what we tend to are examining. Body language can work with us to confirm how somebody feels concerning what they're saying. For instance, an individual could reveal to her manager that she would be glad to consider her body language anyway, showing that she is genuinely in no way, shape, or form upbeat concerning it.

It will be an essential goody that may work with a supervisor confirm who is the best individual to deal with this task. On the off chance that her heart isn't in it, she may make a sufficient showing when another representative may transform this small occupation into a deep-rooted customer. Body language could be the deciding element in a future employee meeting. Suppose the candidate's body language passes on that he's quiet with the topic and passes on certainty. In that case, he contains a higher possibility of acquiring the obligation, especially during this vigorous occupation market. We talked before concerning the very actuality that somebody's language is deciphered as being awkward and crazy. These are some of the very characteristics that formwork candidates show up yet guaranteed and cozy too. In an extreme companionship, one's body language will demonstrate that somebody is focusing or doesn't often think about what the contrary individual says. Inclining forward into the discussion shows that this individual is curious about hearing what the other individual is saying. Reclining would demonstrate that he was unbiased or felt predominant. Inclining forward and standing close while talking may show that somebody is forcefully making an endeavor to guide the other individual or attempting to rule the discussion. Observing somebody while not visually connecting demonstrates that you are not very tuned yet are looking for your opportunity to talk. It offers your companion the inclination that you don't very think often about them and what they need to say and may cause them not to focus cautiously on you when it is your flip to talk in the discussion. You'd say one thing that adds up to 93 % is significant.

Everything You Need to Know About Body Language
Its numbers themselves - regardless of whether a few say it surmised - are greatly amazing. It shows that it is imperative to be advised to examine body language - because the specific message comes from that point. It is, in fact, appallingly important to comprehend what the contrary individual amazingly needs to pass on. Such information would make your life very basic. Most people can "pick up the signs" regardless of whether they don't get a handle on the best way to peruse body language. For instance, you enter a region, and you "handle" regardless of whether they talked something well-disposed or contending concerning a certain something. The body language of individuals in the space will "advise" you the mindset right away, however on the off chance that you were inquired as to why you concluded that you'd not have the option to clarify. Figuring out how to precisely peruse body language could be expertise like a few extraordinary. We as a whole love Sherlock Holmes and his brilliant perception abilities. Criminal investigators, FBI specialists, people working in knowledge and surveillance, gifted speculators, entertainers, and the like, are prepared inside the specialty of perusing body language.

They utilize this expertise to trick you into accepting that they're what they are not. There are numerous signs that your body can send automatically. For instance, you will frown at seeing regurgitation or dung on a plate; you may grin at the image of a little cat playing or blossom sprouting or vehicle or pony hustling with surrender. Understanding what these signs are would work with your control correspondence so you could "communicate" the message you might want to be sent. Knowing to peruse body language would help you: - set up the initiative and keep up it regardless of rivalry; - build up a pleasant and favorable setting officially and casually any place you go; - enhance and enhance your influence powers and along these lines being able to get individuals to do what you wish them to do; - win people's trust; - ensure that you select companions, partners, representatives, and so forth better. These are exclusively a small bunch of benefits you may acquire from figuring out how to check body language. The best is that you'd have the option to stay in the administration of most things since you'd handle not exclusively to peruse elective people's signs however conjointly perceive what signals you should send when and where. Sounds like an idiot-proof formula for accomplishment!

Have you at any point met an ideal outsider and bond? Discovering masses to discuss, you nearly felt as though you had met previously. It felt right. So cozy was you in discussing for all intents and purposes whatever you forgot about time. You grew such a solid bond with that individual that you just understood what he planned to say. Everything just clicked among you, and you felt exceptionally shut to this individual. It might have been an actual fascination, or it might have recently involved being on a similar frequency. You felt your thoughts were in a state of harmony, and you are making the most of your experience with each other. It is affinity. When there is affinity, we tend to contrast our conclusions with somebody else but still feel an association or bond with that individual. The compatibility will even exist between 2 people who share a very couple of similitudes.

Regardless of whether we tend to acknowledge it or not, we tend to continue perusing and being perused by others. Indeed, even while not the expression of words, the language of the body says a lot. Frequently, deciphering body language might be an internal mind factor. We will, in general, may not put forth a reliable attempt to assume through every one of the subtleties why somebody has quite recently collapsed their arms across their chest and limited their eyes at us, anyway by one way or another, this body language enrolls subconsciously and causes us to feel uncomfortable. The psyche promptly deciphers these activities to point to obstruction, doubt, or disdain, regardless of whether we tend to have not made a conscious investigation of the contradicting individual or their experience. Every little thing about you, be it outward or unobtrusive, conveys something to somebody else. The words you use, your outward appearances, what you are doing along with your hands, your manner of speaking, and your degree of eye-to-eye connection will affirm whether people settle for or reject you and your message. To be convincing, you must bless not exclusively transparency yet furthermore authority. Everybody convinces professionally.

Body Language Essentials

There's no methodology around it. Regardless of whether you're a deal gifted, a business person, or maybe a keep-at-home parent, in case you can't persuade others to your way of reasoning, you will be continually abandoned. Get your free reports at Success Advantage to verify that you are not left watching others pass you, making a course for progress. Donald Trump said all that needed to be said, "Study the specialty of influence. Practice it. Build up a comprehension of its significant worth across all parts of life." Using body language to its fullest not exclusively includes dominating your utilization of outward motions to make and look after affinity; however, conjointly involves procuring the capacity to peruse someone else's body language.

At the point when you'll have the option to peruse body language viably, you can build up the feelings and inconvenience of others. You'll see pressure and conflict. You'll have the option to feel dismissal and doubt. It would help if you saw that your body language adds to or brings down your message. In different words, your psyche signals and articulations can either help or hurt your capacity to impact others. You'll make affinity by comprehension and embracing the legitimate body stances and faces for your possibility. Touch is another amazing piece of body language- - sufficiently crucial to give an entire area to it alone. Touch will be a viable mental procedure. Subliminally, we will, in general, really like to be contacted; it causes us to feel appreciated and loved. However, it's actual that we tend to do should know and cautious about a trim level of the populace who aversions being contacted in any capacity. However, in many cases, touch can work with place people agreeable and make them extra open to you and your ideas.

Spot can create a positive insight inside the individual being contacted. Touch envelops great translations of promptness, warmth, similitude, unwinding, and familiarity. In one investigation study, administrators did one of two things when giving back library cards to college understudies looking at books: possibly they didn't contact the individual in any regard during the trade, or they made light-weight, actual contact by putting a hand over the researcher's palm. Constantly, those understudies who were contacted during the exchange evaluated the library administration extra well than individuals who were not contacted by any means. Servers/servers who contacted clients on the arm when inquiring about whether all were well gotten bigger tips and were assessed a ton of well than those who didn't contact their clients. We realize that bound spaces of the body will be openly contacted while various zones are forbidden. Women wouldn't fret being moved by elective ladies, and they're genuinely lenient toward being contacted (fittingly) by men. Men ordinarily wouldn't fret being moved by a new ladylike, yet factors get harder to foresee when men contact various men. When all is said in done, men don't care for being moved by new men. Safe spaces of contact incorporate the shoulders, lower arms and hands, and now and again, the higher back. It all relies upon the case and connection between the two gatherings past to the touch. On the off chance that you have done any preparation in interchanges, public talking, or shows, there is a reasonable probability that body language has been important for the customized. For quite a while, similar to tons, if not thousands, of elective mentors, I've obediently passed on the insight that our correspondence has three parts - words, manner of speaking, and body language. In the same way as other others, I've ascribed the work during this field to Albert Mehrabian and cited the figures of relative significance - body language 55percent, manner of speaking 38%, and words seven. I've clarified on fluctuated events that if somebody is incongruent in their correspondence and their body language is giving a very surprising message from the words, at that point, we'll accept the body language and not the words. I've helped bunches of people create attention to their body language and control their speaking manner to make a more successful general message. Yet, do you perceive what I'd never done work generally as of late? I'd never filter

Mehrabian's unique work! Body language is a critical piece of eye-to-eye correspondence.

A few languages depend a great deal of intensely on it than others to help pass on subtleties of that implies. Local English speakers are less dependent on body language to pass on, which implies that the language's wealth permits us to talk decisively. Local speakers of languages with less serious jargon are commonly astonishing in communicating through tone, pitch, outward appearance, and articulate signals. It is valid, also, that on the off chance that somebody says, 'I need forward to working with you and at the indistinguishable time appearance at the clock and doesn't visually connect, most people can accept that the words were not an outflow of what the individual was truly thinking. In different words, we can accept body language rather than words if the two are giving various messages. However, it uses an instinctual comprehension of body language that we have probably won't be deliberately mindful of. In the indistinguishable methodology, if somebody somehow happened to say, 'I'm attempting forward to working with you in a low droning, with a little murmur toward the end, you most likely wouldn't trust it briefly. Once more, if the manner of speaking is imparting something unique about the words, at that point, we will, in general will, in general, accept the manner of speaking. Passing on the which methods for your message is without question important. How would you do this?

Once more, it appears to be like this basic - through words. On the off chance that the words say one issue and the body language says something different, the body language is accepted as the genuine message. It's regularly said that body language doesn't lie. It is valid because body language is an oblivious cycle deciphered by the legitimate cerebrum of the recipient. It's difficult isn't easier body language because a little variety will mean a few very surprising things to various people. Subsequently, it's critical to understand what your body language is passing on. One can, at the same time, make exact inductions from many-body motions. The eyes and outward appearances pass on most body language messages.

Being a tease might be a generally perceived sort of correspondence. Since the eyes and mouth are the chief unmistakable, it is essential to check how you are doing them while explaining. Facial developments are the second most huge side of body language. The preeminent significant facial development is that of the mouth. Upward turns toward the mouth's side are frequently sure signs and descending turns or level lines in the mouth exhibit cynicism. Notice your lips to decide whether they are squeezed together or loose and cozy. Do they give indications of joy or indications of dissatisfaction? Somebody's cheeks and dimple structure are likewise essential to take a gander at. The first significant thing to see regarding body language is that we keep an eye on all have it- - but some is uncommonly unpretentious. The vast majority yet never give shut consideration to their own or others' body language. Viable correspondence expects you to watch body language as it passes on roughly 58p.c of the message. It would help if you instigated input from others to work out how your conveyance is being seen. Hear a few thoughts from male and female companions, associates, bosses, subordinates, and colleagues. Even though you'll get various responses, an example will arise, giving you an arrangement to 'practice' your introduction while cooperating with explicit individuals or groups. Have you at any point met an ideal outsider and snap? Discovering tons to talk concerning, you practically felt as though you had met previously. It exclusively felt right. So taken were you in chatting with the individual is that you forgot about time.

You grew such a solid bond you understood what he would say before he said it. Everything clicked between every one of you, and you felt pulled into the current individual. It'd be a longing, or it'd have involved simply being on an undifferentiated from recurrence. You felt your thoughts were internal, and you are making the most of your experience with each other. It is frequently known as affinity. Once there's affinity, we will, in general, will disagree in our conclusions with someone else, yet we will, in general, actually feel an alliance or bond with an individual. Liking will even exist between those that share a couple of similitudes exclusively. Regardless of whether we will, in general, unravel it or not, we tend to are unendingly checking and being perused by others. Indeed, even while not utilizing the hear-able correspondence of words, the body's language says a lot. Regularly, deciphering body language may be a psyche issue.

We will, in general, keep an eye on not from an honest exertion to expect through all the little print of why somebody has moved their arms across their chest and limited their eyes at us, in any case, some way or another, this visual correspondence enrolls subconsciously and causes us to feel uncomfortable. The inner mind immediately deciphers these activities to reason opposition, doubt, or resentment, even though we have not made a mindful investigation of the contradicting individual or their experience. Everything concerning you, be it outward or refined, conveys one issue to another person. The words you use, your outward appearances, what you are doing together alongside your hands, your manner of speaking, and your degree of eye-to-eye connection can confirm whether individuals settle for or reject you and your message. To be influential, you should depict receptiveness, yet besides authority.

Chapter 2: How Does Body Language Work

Body language is another term given to the non-verbal correspondence we tend to do with our bodies each day. A lot of our everyday correspondence is considered to be non-verbal. The investigation of body language works by discovering our shifted body motions, eye enlargements, and surprisingly the correction in our voice in certain things. The fundamental reason for body language is that our body's limbic framework or reptilian mind controls our most essential endurance capacities, just as the battle or flight reaction can normally advise our bodies to play out specific signals. Indeed, even infants appear to naturally secure how body language functions and are prepared to impart their necessities to us using their little body motions. Infants gain since the beginning how certain motions get certain reactions. For example, grinning and shifting one's head marginally, for the most part, brings about an ascent in consideration. In any event, learning the best approach to shake one's head "yes" and "no" is by all accounts got from our youth, where the "yes" head gesture permitted us to search out our mom's bosom to take care of from, and the "no" head gesture ends the taking care of interaction. When we are youngsters, body language signs are more obvious because we tend to haven't figured out how to cover them or limit them.

Thus, kids construct magnificent instances of study with regards to non-verbal correspondence. Children, as a rule, have little administration over their responses to fluctuated things; subsequently, when they have a like or hate over something, they ordinarily let you perceive. You will see more characteristic limbic body language signs from youngsters than you would from a grown-up along these lines. For instance, when a kid lies, they tend to stow away orbit their mouths, almost trying to keep the lie from getting away. As we will, in general, get old, we may divert this movement by scratching our nose or going our fingers through our hair. As we become more seasoned, we gain proficiency with the best approach to cover our faces and developments. In these cases, body language works by learning the pieces of the body we will, in general, have almost no to no administration over, and the pieces of the body that we for the most part don't focus on. It implies that the seeing of our feet, understudy enlargements, and the pitch of our voices. Our feet are one of only a handful of few pieces of the body we don't focus on except if we incline tore deliberately considering them. Subsequently, the feet are where individuals contemplating body language will begin.

Interpreting Body Language
They will reveal to you who the prevailing individual is in the relationship, regardless of whether somebody is curious about you. On the off chance that somebody is acquiring arranged to withdraw. Student expansion is another body language sign saw to check whether somebody prefers or abhorrence something. Be that as it may, this reaction exclusively endures quickly subsequently, except if you are sufficiently close to notice their underlying reaction to an obvious

improvement, you will miss seeing the understudy expansions. Likewise, our vocal pitch is one thing we will, in general, ought to know about since our voice frequently mirrors the feelings, we have an inclination tore feeling. For example, when focused on numerous person's voices will begin to increment in pitch. On the off chance that somebody's pitch doesn't change when they're expressing one thing that ought to have a passionate reaction identified with it, at that point which will be an indication of trickery. Since you know how the investigation of body language functions, the resulting time you adventure out, set aside the effort to notice everyone around you and see what you'll translate from their body language signs. Just make sure that you are not very clear in others' perceptions, making people awkward around you and revising their body language signs. Imparting is one in every one of the most fundamental things we do throughout everyday life.

Because of its numerous perspectives, it's also profoundly powerless against confusion. Consequently, it is a decent arrangement to claim as bountiful mindfulness about it as achievable - not exclusively to be all the more comprehended - any way to extra unmistakably see others, correspondingly. Tragically, an assortment of the principal amazing parts of correspondence is normally unseen deliberately, considerably less utilized with authority. They fall into the class of body language. I've seen superfluously shocking outcomes with witnesses deficiently set up in attitude or body language in my Witness Preparation

Service. Numerous individuals essentially don't comprehend the unintended messages we tend to remove sending. Whether with family, companions, rivals, associates, public talking, or doing such things as giving legitimate declaration - it's important to comprehend what we tend to are passing on every moment. Even after we're quiet, our body language is communicating. Furthermore, when we do talk, our simple words are exclusively 50% of the message. The rest we express in our tone.

A few moms have been known to alert, 'Don't utilize that manner of speaking with me!' In the last part of the 1800's, the now incredible Charles Darwin composed The Expression of the Emotions in Man and Animals. It turned into the most punctual known logical investigation into what has gotten alluded to as body language (counting nonverbal correspondence) and conduct, frequently commented in people as "disposition." Subsequently, there has been an amazing measure of examining the sorts, articulations, and impacts of each spoken and implicit correspondence and conduct. While these signs are frequently consequently sensitive that we're not deliberately alert to them, research has distinguished a huge choice. In contrast to Darwin, in this content, we'll be zeroing in exclusively on mankind.

Understand Yourself
Nonetheless, to the shame of humankind, it's cost taking note of that creatures to appear to be bountiful

more adroit at apparent and non-verbal correspondence than a few of us people. Accordingly, what will body language mean, and how would we, in general, remember it? Will having arms crossed counsel exclusively somebody is shielding herself or obstructing others from acquiring excessively close, just like the last suspicion? May it likewise mean the individual is truly awkward, similar to cold, or in torment? Could it mean she might be terrified? Or then again likely furious? What's more, what in regards to moving eyes or not setting up eye to eye connection? These are ordinarily seen as demonstrative of deceitfulness., imagine a scenario where the individual is genuinely back. Maybe confounded? Or then again, maybe terrified? Since private development and brain science have been promoted since the 1970s, body language examination has developed extensively. By and by, after the distribution of Julius Fast's acclaimed book, Body Language, public media and surprisingly some accordingly called "subject matter experts" actually spend significant time excessively worked on the translation of guarded appearing stances like arm-intersection and leg-crossing. While these nonverbal practices can demonstrate sure emotions and perspectives, research doubtlessly shows that body language is a lot of a ton of fragile, diverse, and less conclusive than initially recognized. Body language and voice tone commonly convey more data about translation (or confusion) than words do.

Hence, it bodes well to see, recognize, and explicit these with as great transparency as possible. To some degree, body language alludes to the nonverbal signs we tend to so normally unwittingly use. They develop an enormous extent of our correspondence (or miscommunication), from outward appearances to body developments and positions, to what we will, in general, don't say or how we do say a certain something. Not understanding what we have an inclination to be passing on or what another person is saying through body language and speaking denies us of knowledge and comprehension - and maybe much bigger happiness regarding life. Vital for clear understanding is contemplating a few signals. For instance, conditions of given things and conditions - and to get to signals in a bunch of gathering, rather than having some expertise in a solitary motion (like crossed arms) or vocal tone. As astounding as it might appear, an unprecedented number of studies have moderately discovered that, by and large, we watch out for people to answer around sixty % of our correspondence exclusively by unraveling nonverbal messages.

Voice resonance comprises about another 27 %- - while the leftover humble 13% of what we tend to answer are the specific words. Somebody will disclose to us they love us while utilizing a snarling manner of speaking - and we will, in general, ever trust them. We will, in general, constantly answer a large number of nonverbal prompts and practices, including stances, outward appearances (with miniature muscle developments and progressive changes in skin tinge), eye developments, signals, and vocal tones. Indeed, even our outward appearances influence us! Have a go at remaining displeased while grinning comprehensively and strolling energetically. From our handshakes to how we tend to walk, stand, sit, to the garments we will in general wear- - nonverbal subtleties uncover more concerning us than we would conceivably comprehend. We utilize these equivalent signs when we decipher and identify with others, ordinarily, unknowingly. Luckily, we tend to will everlastingly improve. Figuring out how to more readily decipher and convey without words and how we say something might be a great strategy to propel others' comprehension and acquire our message across a ton of viably. Here are a few things to mull over: Generally talking, outward appearances at first have the most importance.

Mull over the different information in a distracted or objecting scowl, gripped teeth, a splendid grin, or the plan for a despondency-ridden face. All we will in general need to do is flip on the television with the sound quieted - and paying little mind to where it is in the globe, articulations for satisfaction, delicacy, frustration, melancholy, outrage, and concern are all-inclusive and clear to see. Eye stare is another imperative nonverbal conduct. Looking or abstaining from looking, gazing, or routinely attempting endlessly all have powerful messages. In any event, squinting, which is frequently very oblivious, has social ramifications. A few investigations have shown that when individuals experience someone else or things they like, the pace of squinting will increment, and understudies widen. On the other hand, needing at somebody and flickering very only will mean hostility or- - very actually - riveted consideration. As a rule, entertainers with incredible screen presence hold watchful eyes while squinting only sometimes and gradually.

Common Patterns of Interpreting Behavior
The contrasting ramifications are inside the going with facial muscles. Taking a gander at someone else will show a scope of feelings, just as aggression, interest, and fascination. Motions like waving, pointing, and utilizing finger developments and signs are fundamental ways to pass on importance. The power and stream of how we utilize our arms, hands, and fingers counsel a decent arrangement - from moving to being decided, from attempting offers of incorporation and harmony to aggression stances. Stroking another's brow passes on mindful, while a grasped clenched hand loans a unique message. Paralinguistics alludes to vocal correspondence going with real verbally expressed words. It incorporates manners of speaking, volume, affectation, meter, and pitch. When something is said in a, to some degree, reliable manner of speaking, audience members may decipher endorsement and energy. One thing said significantly more persuasively, or discreetly, will effectively suggest cruelty or maybe danger.

The indistinguishable words said during a reluctant manner of speaking would potentially show disarray, absence of certainty, objection, or absence of interest. A convey at the tip, likewise with an inquiry, passes on a completely entirely unexpected message. Stance can pass on an amicable arrangement of data. Depending on the setting, slumping will be deciphered in various manners by which. During a gathering, it will pass on easygoing unwinding or irreverence; in a very court, it, for the most part, without a doubt, can be viewed as the last mentioned. Inclining forward might demonstrate revenue and energy or animosity and terrorize. Solid military strolling may derive the absence of affectability. Proxemics is one of the extra refined anyway, exceptionally rehearsed parts of body language. It alludes to the number of houses around us we tend to expect in shifting conditions. People regularly ask about their requirement for an "individual house." The amount of distance we tend to require and the amount of house we comprehend as having a place with us is impacted by a scope of elements, just as accepted practices, situational factors (like riding on the tram), character attributes, and level of commonality.

For example, the quantity of individual houses required while having a casual discussion with someone else changes between eighteen creeps to four or five feet. Except if we incline tore in a packed gathering or lifted, being drawn nearer by somebody we don't see well who comes at stretches ten crawls of us is normally taken to be obtrusive. The personal discussion has adequate space from 0 to twelve inches or extra. Then again, the space expected while visiting with a horde of individuals is around 6 to 12 feet, depending on the get-together and set size. Touch, or "haptics," is another vital segment of nonverbal conduct. A lot of examination has focused on the significance of touch in early stages and youth conduct advancement. Harry Harlow's notable investigation of monkeys exhibited how the hardship of touch and address obstructs full and sound events. Child monkeys raised by wire moms experienced lasting shortfalls in conduct and social collaboration. The equivalent has been seen in human infants and children.

The hardship of personal touch breeds levels of partition. After we see how people nibbled one another, this offers us numerous hints to think about. look is how we decide to bless ourselves; regardless of whether we care, almost no or a load keeps being imparting. Tones, styles of apparel, decoration, or the deficiency thereof, what we wear our hair and various variables meaning for appearance, make motions toward people. Wearing pants for a proper occasion or to a court contains an entirely unexpected message at that point dropping by the neighborhood café. Exploring shading brain research shows that various tones will determine temperaments and reactions, contingent upon the general public.

Universal Gestures

The look can likewise impact physiological responses, judgment, and translations. Consider the appearances of pop stars versus reporters. In its differed and rich structures, language might be a blessing. It serves us well to require some investment in noticing and rehearsing the make-from attitude, just as voice tones and nonverbal body language. Information is only a start. Applying it considers authority. It's the contrast between hypothesis and notice. Keep in mind that extra right comprehension of others' body language needs considering a different of signs. In calm conditions, and when strategically done, deciding the exactness of an understanding can be supported by confirming our insight with the other party. Working with this could be charming and intriguing. Its mindfulness and expertise will help everybody figure out how to peruse various people a great deal of dependably and upgrade our capacity to talk extra adequately.

It may even improve our lives. Regardless of whether you remember it or not, the visual correspondence might be a generous issue in charge of. Yet, everybody you meet arrives at an oblivious starting assessment concerning you. In a few callings fundamentally in callings any place you work with and help others, listening abilities are a prerequisite and vital for making great connections with your customers/patients. Whether or not you work with people to keep up their connections, which offers direction to individuals for satisfaction in business, or insight people like youngsters, guardians, couples, etc., they are seeing and surveying your visual correspondence. Showing good listening abilities makes individuals simpler and extra open to share. Poor visual correspondence may cause you to miss out on fundamental things. It is so imperative to you! You ought to be mindful of every word thoroughly and sincerely. Your visual correspondence produces what others feel is basic, like giving them the consideration contact they have. Here it's fundamental to understand what the indications of a helpless listener are, and you should attempt to free yourself of any of these. In case you're inside, the propensity for keeping your arms collapsed up over your chest, else you tap your toes with eagerness, lean or address to some of the time, or look to a great extent constantly while tuning in, at that point, you're telling the other individual that you're not interested about what the person in question is saying to you. It might bring about an unmistakable stage in correspondence and may cause imperative misfortunes in business.

Subsequently, how would it be a good idea for you to respond, with the goal that your visual correspondence begins to convey positive messages to the individual you're conversing with? Introductory off, you should endeavor and face the contrary individual solidly on. Try not to hope to convey a positive message. At that point, we will, in general, address the situation of your body at the hour of correspondence. It would help if you accepted an agreeable and open stance. It would help if you never remained your arms or legs collapsed; the contrary individual will suggest that you don't seem, by all accounts, to be keen on focusing on their motivation. Assuming you slender forward while addressing somebody, your visual correspondence says that you truly are giving further consideration to spoken discourse. In qualification, inclining away shows that you essentially have no interest in what along these lines ever. At that point, we will, in general, return to the issue of eye-to-eye connection. Eye to eye connection is the one among the principal, if not the most, vital issue. Attempt to keep in touch regularly. Assuming you continue needing down or looking ceaselessly, you just appear to show any interest in the exchange and feel awkward.

The significance of a casual stance can't be overemphasized anyway an equilibrium should be reached. Try not to endeavor and be excessively solid. Neither must you be excessively formal while conversing with somebody. Simultaneously, try not to be so loose or casual that it verges on the sting of haughtiness or incivility. That great equilibrium of a loose and loosened-up pose helps release your correspondence accomplice up and empower them. In case you feel that you have endured gigantic misfortunes in the past attributable to your poor visual correspondence, at that point, you should start to follow up on the data named underneath.

Basic Rules for Body Language
For each understanding of body language, it is important to dedicate consideration regarding the scope of pivotal rules that data subsequently the significance, everything being equal, signals, and articulations (and the decisions you make in regards to them). The translations you'll discover in the resulting sections are exclusively right in sixty to 80 percent of circumstances, on the off chance that they happen independently or in separation. On the off chance that you see a bound development happen repeatedly, the likelihood is greater than the understanding is right. On the off chance that among a brief timeframe, you see a combination of 3 to 5 developments that everyone gives an undifferentiated signal, you'll have the option to reach your inference with a deep level of sureness. On the off chance that somebody contacts the tip of his nose once all through a discussion, it very well may be that he has a bothersome nose. In any case, if all through a 2-minute time frame somebody contacts his nose, rubs his eyes, covers his mouth, makes a stride in reverse, keeps away from eye-to-eye connection, and folds his arms, at that point there's a reasonable probability that he either discovers matters unpleasant or that he's lying. If you must decide between what you hear (words) and what you see (developments), it is smarter to accept what you see.

The body makes up for the things that are said. It's feasible to set up a misrepresentation or cover pressure for a brief timeframe, yet taking everything into account. It's substantially more intense to stow away or distort critical information. Why? Our body intuitively shows on a superficial level what's going on within. Fluctuated examines shown that our limbic framework works quicker than our forces of sane idea; articulations and signals will, in general, educate reality before we tend to will deliberately change our conduct. Its cognizant change is multiple times slower than the wild signals of the limbic framework. What people are encountering inside will, along these lines, be noticeable remotely. The converse is genuine still: After you see somebody with an outward appearance that is not troubled, it's profoundly conceivable that this individual isn't encountering misery at that point. In any case, you need to consider head assortment 5: If this individual never includes a tragic facial component, even occasionally when you realize that she is encountering despair, you should change your decisions. All through our instructional classes, we tend to are generally asked: If somebody ordinarily folds his arms, will this mean he includes a shut demeanor? What do you think? Is the answer for the current inquiry indeed, or no?

For instance, somebody remaining outside in the focal point of winter who has failed to remember her jacket could horrendously well have her arms crossed. Anyway, this simply implies that she is cold. At the indistinguishable time, she may ideally be directing a charming and exciting discussion along with her companions! Be that as it may, what might be said about somebody wearing a specialist's dress and examining one thing with an associate in an emergency clinic hall? Clinics are generally warm so that for this situation, the crossed arms, in all probability, make them a thing to attempt to do with the personality of the discussion. You wish to give careful consideration to the situation, things, and the individual's climate about whom you might want to make inferences. We persistently endeavor to try not to make understandings dependent on a solitary photo. On the off chance that you have no places of correlation, your decisions will be less precise. To shape dependable ends, what we investigate for most importantly are monstrous and powerful changes in body language positions. For instance, on the off chance that somebody unexpectedly places his legs in a really banter position all through an exchange, while he, in any case, seems loose, this has a ton of greater that implies than if he has his legs in the contention position from the beginning of the conversation. Timing is likewise exceptionally essential: A significant change in body language position exactly when a shiny new worth is referenced says a lot more than if a similar development is made at an unbiased second inside the discussion.

After we give understandings of that way to a signal like contacting your nose, we tend to generally hear individuals say: "Indeed, anyway, I routinely chewed the tip of my nose once I am talking. Everybody in my family will do it., it doesn't mean we are lying!" It may be valid: After applying the fifth essential rule contacting the nose could lose its customary understanding. Give careful consideration to the propensities for the individual you're translating just as to developments that are "conventional" for somebody in the particular situation. On the off chance that somebody has built up a specific development as a propensity over a scope of years, customary understandings of this development given in the subsequent sections won't be right. If, for instance, somebody is, as a rule, prone to grin, in any event, when she is feeling antagonistic, at that point, you can't naturally decipher this present individual's grin as an indication of happiness. To realize that developments, signals, and articulations you wish to prohibit from your translation as problematic, you first need to look at an adequate scope of things to build up this present individual's propensities. Far beyond propensities, outside factors like taking prescription or medications, utilizing liquor, or having motion modifying medicines like a corrective medical procedure or Botox would all be able to play an undertaking. By assessing a person's propensities, you can stay away from botches like disentangling a genuine articulation of pleasure as a statement of hatred.

How Body Language Depicts Emotions
The corroborative gesture traces back to medieval times. In a few societies, the short descending bow of the apex is an indication of regard. Our day-by-day discussions show that we tend to make do with and consider what the other individual is saying. There are,

nonetheless, various exemptions. Like in Bulgaria, where gesturing the head implies no. Also, in Japan, it proposes that somebody is listening meticulously, however not concurring. In Western nations, where we are a great deal used to showing our emotions plainly, the zenith's affirming gesture signals endorsement, particularly when it goes with happily. On the off chance that somebody gestures their head, it can conjointly imply excitement about the thing you're saying. As some time in the past as 1989, Rimland and Jones stressed that showing a positive response of this sort to your discussion accomplice's expressions assists with supporting great correspondence. In business settings, it will be useful to keep an eye fixed out for the corroborative gestures of the individual you are conversing with. The head ordinarily main gesture offers a veritable answer, regardless of whether a "no" shake trails it just minutes after the fact. When this occurs, it could imply that the individual requirements to cover his positive answer, maybe as an arranging strategy.

As you have effectively learned, unconstrained body language won't ever lie. A brief and oblivious "yes" gesture can uncover somebody's positive assessment in even the warmest conversations. At the point when a child is currently not eager, it shakes its head. Turning the head from feature to side on the neck is the best way to show no in things of this sort, which is why this development has procured the importance of refusal or forswearing in many societies. A similar development will likewise be utilized once we experience the feeling of shock when one thing astounding occurs, or our discussion accomplice shocks us.

Nonetheless, while breaking down this motion, it's urgent to recall our five essential interpretive standards. In different conditions, shaking the apex can have an extremely surprising that implies or is just a way to stretch the feelings an individual encounter. In the past section, we tend to referenced how placing things into your mouth can be a sign of frailty. However, this motion can conjointly happen when somebody is placed under tension or puts herself under pressure. When we were youthful young people, we tend to get a pacifier to put in our mouths to make us quit crying. A pacifier represents a sensation of wellbeing. It clarifies why a few grown-ups still think that it's soothing to put something in their mouths at extreme minutes. They do this unknowingly to have a sense of security. Placing your fingers in your mouth is an outward articulation of an inward requirement for security. In any case, it doesn't need to be fingers: Cigarettes, pens, and the arm of your glasses would all be able to serve a similar capacity.

Contacting your hair with your hand will be an indication of bashfulness or anxiety. It is regularly not a cutting-edge propensity and will be seen in numerous new societies. Today, you would potentially see it, for example, when a supervisor is driving visitors around her organization interestingly and isn't positive about how they are visiting. The equivalent is valid about somebody who is presenting a substitution project at a fundamental gathering. During an entirely unexpected setting, women would conceivably play with their hair to attract the consideration of or express their advantage in a very man, particularly when it's in an attractive look. Scratching your head can indicate concern or vulnerability concerning something you wish to specify or do, strikingly if you scratch with the right hand. (The right hand is associated with the objective left of the cerebrum.) By scratching your head alongside your right hand, you show that you don't comprehend the answer for something and might want to work with it. On the off chance that you make a similar motion along with your left hand (associated with the passionate right 0.5 of your cerebrum), this shows that at the appropriate time, you will, in all likelihood, understand the arrangement all alone. In different words, lefthanded scratching signals transitory vulnerability rather than a might want for work with. Inbound circumstances, scouring your jaw can be a sign of uncertainty. For instance, when somebody offering a response is uncertain about the impression, he is making on his audience members. You see the indistinguishable signal when somebody who wants to introduce a choice reflects absurd made to him. In these conditions, be paying special mind to various signs which will demonstrate either a positive or negative reaction.

Body Language Signs

Depending on the body language that goes with the jawline scouring, you'll have the option to presumably reason a nonverbal choice before your discussion accomplice opens his mouth to talk. As we tend to found in the past part, covering your mouth makes a hindrance to correspondence. Be that as it may, there are different ways you'll have the option to place your hand before your mouth, and they each convey an alternate message. We will generally contemplate the signal where the palm level is squeezed against the lips, with the fingers loose and unfurl during this segment. Its signal could imply that the individual is uncertain concerning something. Moreover, it will imply that an individual has said she laments right away or will be utilized to communicate conflict with one thing that somebody else has said. If somebody is lying and encounters pressure like this, it is possible that placing his hand before his mouth unknowingly puts him a ton of loose because people will see it less simple to peruse the dread in his face.

Covering the mouth will likewise happen in different things: for instance, when you get outstandingly risky or deplorable news. It applies when we see a mishap or something hazardous. The circumstance, the situating, and the way of setting the hand will permit you to separate between the signal's entirely unexpected implications. At the point when somebody feels tragic or inept whenever they have said or done one thing inappropriate, they can immediately bring down their eyes, as though they need at the floor. It communicates a sensation of vulnerability and anxiety, during which they presently don't have any desire to appear to be their discussion accomplice in the eye. It looking away will likewise happen, for example, when a lesser individual from staff out of the blue meets the large chief. By observing intently for this eye development, you'll become familiar with a ton concerning the remaining of different people among a gathering. If somebody hunches their back at a given second, this could flag an absence of inspiration for additional contact. It could reflect negative feelings toward the discussion accomplice, quite if the slumping stance is amidst an extreme look and a brought down (or raised) head. If you might want to respond strongly to the current sort of unrivaled body language, you'll have the option to counter the slumping by pushing your chest forward. Something contrary to slumping is pushing your shoulders back in this way that your chest is pushed forward extra obviously. It signs bigger receptiveness for contact and an eagerness to think with interest and a spotlight. You typically see this in the road when somebody meets somebody they like.

Pushing your shoulders back shows excitement and good emotions. We looked at this in the past section. Like a turtle that pulls out its head into its shell when it's apprehensive, a few people attempt to bring down their heads between their raised shoulders. The strained shoulders shield the neck, uncovering feelings that produce a sensation of stress and a might want for protection. When somebody tenses their shoulders during this methodology, it will also imply that they need to separate themselves from valid. It licenses us to see that any discussion does not inspire them. Possibly they feel overpowered and need your opportunity to recuperate their poise. You'll have the option also to see this equivalent stance in certain people with sorrow. On the contrary, it would perhaps imply that an individual is discouraged (or even only cold) because sorrow might be a cool feeling. All through that, there's almost no energy coursing inside the body. Stress is also a cool feeling that can give us goosebumps instead of the warm feeling of outrage, which makes us red inside the face. Allowing your shoulders to hang could be an indication of a give-up and shortcoming. You can see this, for instance, when a sales rep needs to answer to his supervisor that he has recently lost a genuine customer and knows about there is no way to win that client back.

People utilize this signal to the point that they presently don't have any interest in proceeding with a discussion. It passes on apathy and a shortage of conviction. You may see this, for example, when you are endeavoring to impact somebody to take on a troublesome undertaking. By shrugging his shoulders, the other individual shows that he thinks you are asking one thing irrationally and that he isn't prepared to acknowledge your contentions and complaints.

A similar motion will likewise connote a shortage of ability to make a call. It might be that the individual included doesn't get a handle on the arrangement. In these conditions, shrugging the shoulders could be an offer of bothering. It is likewise utilized as a reaction to something you would prefer not to hear. We prior talked about fastening your hands as a sign of dissatisfaction. It can likewise be an approach to conceal your disquiet in certain unique circumstances: for instance, all through an important meeting or when you're stressed concerning something. It can conjointly cover a negative point. You'll have the option to decipher this situation in a few manners by which, contingent upon the specific circumstance and valid. For instance, somebody may lay elbows on the table and hold her fastened hands before her face. Or on the other hand, the fastened hands would conceivably be laid on the table or held under the stomach (when the individual is standing). Whatever the position, the whiter you'll have the option to find in their knuckles, the more prominent the feelings of dissatisfaction.

A soccer player can rub her hands together when she sees a colleague requiring an extra shot and anticipates a positive outcome. A car sales rep can rub his hands together when a customer consents to look for another Mercedes. In these various settings, the speed with which the hands are scoured is huge. If somebody rubs his hands together rapidly, this is regularly useful for everybody; in general, we will be satisfied with the outcome. Assuming. Nonetheless, the auto sales rep exclusively anticipates that the result should benefit himself (for instance, a genuine commission on the deal that works to the customer's drawbacks). He can presumably rub his hands all the more gradually. It can be the signal you'll have the option to, as a rule, see utilized by the "baddies" in ongoing movies and kid's shows while they're cooking up their next fiendish arrangement. Holding your wrist might be an indication of dissatisfaction and an undertaking at discretion. The motion can be made either before or behind the body. At the point when it's made at the front, it additionally frames an arm boundary.

When it is made behind the back, it's less recognizable thus more positive toward others. On the off chance that the hand on the wrist you are grasping is balled, this normally flags stifled bothering. The wrist that is being grasped is also critical. Is it the left wrist associated with the mind's passionate right, or is it the correct wrist, associated with the normal left 0.5 of the cerebra? What's more, the upper the hand on the wrist and a ton of squeezed the individual's overall stance, the more noteworthy their feeling of dissatisfaction, particularly if the arms are held behind the back.

On the off chance that an individual's hands are shaking, this can be a clear sign that they encounter incredible feelings. It might be stifled concern, which you'll have the option to by and large see in apprehensive speakers before they start an introduction or controlled resentment during a warmed conversation or exchange. Another variety of this motion includes rapid and turbulent developments, albeit the that implies extensively the indistinguishable. Turbulent hand developments give the impression of incongruence-a shortage of understanding between the body and, in this manner, the words being expressed. Accordingly, they are an indication of apprehension. The hands and the wrists assume an indispensable part in our nonverbal correspondence. It's accordingly a good sign when your discussion accomplice has loosened up wrists because this reflects transparency and interest in what you must refer to. When the accomplice talks, it implies positive aims, consideration for the other, and a decreased impulse to persuade.

The root of this positive affiliation is situated in how the wrists are loosened up when stroking or showing actual affectability giving the signal isn't balanced by various more negative developments and motions. The other of loosened-up wrists is firm and jerky hand developments. It could demonstrate a shortage of commonality or great relations between discussion accomplices. It will conjointly be a sign of strain and stress when somebody needs to remain a tight hang on feelings all through a conversation.

Chapter 3: Powerful Body Language Tips
Another fundamental tip concerning visual correspondence is that you should acknowledge heartily and immovably. Then, we tend to get back to the decision of the seat to plunk down are. You need not show that you basically can't sit except if the contrary individual asks you to. All things being equal, you should choose the essential relevant seat and sit quickly. Be that as it may, never play out the mistake of sitting excessively close or too route from the customer. What distance you need to keep relies upon the demeanor of the customer. A contracting self-observer can want to plunk down at a different distance than a partner-friendly individual.

However, the appropriate length is between twenty to fifty inches. You'll lean forward to ask the customer closer once endeavoring to put weight on a particular reason. Eye to eye connection is a crucial portion of visual correspondence. Eye-to-eye connection. Open eye to eye connection and needing around here and there finished and once more will send the message that you simply need more trust in yourself. However, try not to consistently look at the other individual, which may cause the customer to feel very awkward. Ceaselessly endeavor to talk in your distinctive voice. If your voice is brimming with enthusiasm, it'll work in a flash to command the customer's notice. Correspondence through visual correspondence has been happening for more than 1,000,000 years; in any case, it's exclusively been experimentally concentrated to any degree at stretches the most recent twenty years or hence; it turned out to be popular all through the Seventies and acquired great notoriety. By the start of this century, it was 'found' by people worldwide, and I anticipate that this tremendously affects human correspondence and formal training. Its book has filled in as a little prologue to body languages, and that I urge you to search for additional hotspots for your investigation and information. Eventually, social orders are your best examination and research facility.

- Cautiously notice your activities which of different people. It is without a doubt the best way for every individual to see the value in a far higher comprehension of the correspondence behaviors that most people find acceptable generally progressed and drawing in monster man himself. Having an astoundingly exceptional stance conveys a strong message to everybody around you that you're interesting and beguiling.
- Everybody can note and build up you as not a middle individual. Looking at somebody in an extremely lady's specific situation, a lady now and then can consider whether a guy is alluring or not by discerning the methodology they stand and walk. The man that displays the recognized stance will champion and rule her awareness because he's the one she'll be keen on. Rising stance is in this manner named because of I the ascending position for a couple of reasons.

- Most regularly, fruitful individuals will utilize this capacity to lift their present resources over the ineffective ones. As of now, by just recognizing that everybody envelops a stance with the possibility of transforming this into a magnificent and, you'll presently ascend to a more elevated level or remain by abusing your situation for your potential benefit. Ascending by abuse with one among your most prominent resources - your stance. Somebody grins parts will come in general prompt delight from another positive outcome on others than somebody who is typically extreme or disappointed. Grinning is maybe one among the principal vital pieces of visual correspondence; we will, in general, will in general have.
- Most people perceive the strong impact of a genuine, fair grin. A few wonders, especially when it is accurately done. While individuals will light up your heart with a genuine excellent grin, elective people fabricate an awkward sensation in you with their grins. The last one is that we will, in general, condemn in light of the bogus and hopeless grin.
- It's not how you might want to be connected. A bogus grin is generally extra topsy-turvy than a genuine grin, and it keeps going longer.
- It sort of grin starts from the individual who's grinning, however not feeling upbeat or energized towards the contrary individual they are with. For you to try not to show this sort of grin, you'll

invigorate your feelings by building the correct feelings at spans and one small step at a time similar unmitigated sentiment on the skin.

- By communicating your radiant feelings from the inside to the skin, the glow of your legit genuine grin will gradually start to ascend higher and better. Its certified fuel grin will light a little fire and gradually heat up and light up the surrounding space. Start this by keeping in touch with somebody for two seconds.
- At that point, fan the flames of your grin step by step by starting with a next to no grin, and along these lines, gradually enhance it more than 3 seconds till it turns into an expansive grin. It can take an aggregate of five seconds from your underlying eye to eye connection to your broadest grin.

How to Impress Anyone Quickly

The true grin can never-endingly appear to be straightforward and genuine because of you not just removing on a giggle from nothing anyway upon eye-to-eye connection with someone else. What you are doing here is you hang tight for a couple of moments and afterward start grinning, trailed by expanding your grin gradually over various additional seconds for the total outcome. It can bring extra huge outcomes by rehearsing your grins heretofore before a mirror. The extra you grin from inside, the more characteristic it can return to you. A legitimate earnest grin will light up the setting you are in, ease up the climate, and makes certain to rebuild you into a meaningful individual, all the while not talking a word. Interestingly, it is conjointly fun and gigantic to endeavor. Realizing an approach to utilize the pretty eye to eye connection is out and away from the main incredible and quickest course to upsurge your fascination and pull in the other gender into falling overwhelmed with passion for you.

The visual correspondence signals from your eye-to-eye connection can tell the elective individual you're phenomenal, intriguing, and out of the norm. The procedure principally starts with expanding extra eye to eye connection with those you might want to look further interesting. We must tend to make a somewhat strong impression in those underlying couple of seconds of eye-to-eye connection. You may need to focus on here to unendingly explore the individual a touch longer when contrasted with the length of your time you usually elegant look. As you're attempting ceaselessly, envision your eyes stripping off the individual like a cement sticker being stripped taken out from its base surface. Continue to keep in touch for a modest quantity while longer, and in this way, gradually strip your eyes off the individual as you switch. Remember that the force of this technique fluctuates on the individual and their standpoint around then.

Periodically, a way more grounded eye to eye connection is made through associations between ladies to ladies and ladies to men when contrasted with men to men. Tough eye to eye connection is one among the ascribes of closeness and closeness, and that they're the sentiments women wish to aptitude once they are in holds with others. You might be prepared to effectively tell by needing the quantity of your time they pay on the telephone. Later on, various occasions from in some unknown time will become points to talk worried for quite a long time and in progress. When it includes a call between an irregular individual to singular, it will conventionally be over in two or three minutes or two as their discourse has no further evenhanded. All through a discussion with a lady, the communication's closeness level is really serious once a sturdy eye to eye connection is started. At the point when an ordinary companion, associate, or a possible accomplice, they will appear in a flash notification, you extra captivating and agreeable and turn out to be any attracted to you. Applying the room charming eyes method, never-endingly remember to connect for a touch longer before you turn away visually. When you are confronting the woman, you show up moreover captivating as well. If you are a man cooperating with another person, you will try not to misuse sturdy eye-to-eye connection. Unreasonably solid eye to eye connection with another person will just come backtrack as gazing, and regularly this could be shown as violent conduct.

The person's normal response towards this motion is only indistinguishable as however ladies communicating closeness in their discussions. Thus, during this case, for a chap interfacing with another person, you essentially should form an eye-to-eye connection regarding little of the time. The dazzling issue is that you just can, in any case, utilize the scratching mental picture strategy on another fellow and return off as an intriguing individual. Practice makes great, and accordingly, the extra you notice, the higher your abilities are, and hence a ton of common it can become to you. Whenever, keep on making sure to need underneath thought the way of life, environmental factors, situation, and, in this manner, the individual you are associating with once putting these abilities to utilize. Magnificence, as they're saying, is inside the consideration of the onlooker. Drawing in people are people who are dedicated to themselves.

Body Language- Speaking Without Words
Those individuals are precisely generous and beguiling, for they conjure this genuine inclination in their families, companions, and sweethearts, every one of whom can feel furthermore unique thus. Trench yourself, open your heart, brain, and body to the occasion. Thus, the moment is yours. Since you have found out such a great amount about body language, permit us to notice a few focuses that will work with advance throughout everyday life. Here are not many direct the by horrendously amazing tips that may work before the opposition. Before you enter a space where you need to have the legitimate effect or meet somebody you wish to intrigue, take a long and full breath. At the point when you do this, the muscles of your jaw, neck, and shoulder would unwind, furnishing you with a characteristic stance - as opposed to an

unbending and bogus one. The traditional look would have you better than an aggressive look that had you strolled in with unbending neck and shoulder muscles (inflexible because you were on edge). People are instinctually attracted to development. When you move, the eyes right away become focused on you - and with the eyes, your cerebrum. Thus, to stand out and hold it, move through your talk or fabricate an introduction. To ensure most consideration, move for a little time to stop and convey the assertion you need. People peruse the palms down sign as power.

Henceforth, when you need people to focus on you and accept you as a conclusive and straightforward individual, all you must attempt to do is use signals that get your palms to turn downwards. It is particularly significant if your vibe unequivocally regards anything and needs to make a gigantic arrangement out of it. At gatherings or in conversation bunches, the person who talks early is recognized as fundamental and decisive. It is because to start with. Many people feel they need time to heat up before offering their input and consequently appreciate the individuals who talk early are pursued as pioneers in minor methods. Measure the Readiness of Your Audience If the individual is entranced by what you need to refer to, and he would sink once more into the seat and accept a casual position, i.e., He is prepared to think to you persistently. On the off chance that the individual isn't intrigued, he would get himself ready to actuate up and go. On the off chance that this occurs, you should either wrap up what you must say rapidly or alteration the subject and see whether you'll catch the individual's or the crowd's consideration and interest. Before you tackle arrangements, you should test the water a bit. It's continually best to deal when now is the ideal opportunity to encourage the best result. To see out if that is a happy time, test the affinity you have set up with the others utilizing body language. Permit us to say you are situated at a gathering table. Confronting one in every one of the people (or more) lean eliminated from him pushing your seatback. Much of the time, you'll see that the contrary individual also would pretty much mirror your activities. It is how you distance somebody. To take him back to the interface, all you must attempt to do is lean towards the individual now and guarantee that hands are obvious, with one of the two palms confronting upwards. Study him, and blaze a genuine grin. It would be exceptionally uncommon that you'd not get a quick agreeable response from the other individual.

On the off chance that you are prepared to influence the individual along these lines - it is the best and ideal opportunity to talk about regardless of your wish to trade. You would win. concerning significance position is. When you wish to make an official statement that everybody should tune in and comply, augment your position, take a full breath, keep the two-foot firm on the base, understand the breadth and in and hence the tranquility and focusing it brings you. When you are loose and utilize this position, the voice would come out extra thunderous and more profound. A certain position and deep voice are the formulae for the best degree of influence capacity. When you ace this kind of position, few would have the option to oppose your appeal.

Chapter 4: Body Language in Our Daily Life

Body language is muddled enough when you're dealing with people from your way of life, not to mention those from elective components of the reality where social contrasts may include for a store close to home and gifted correspondence. Because things will in this manner effectively turn out badly because of false impressions or coincidental errors, it very well may be valuable to examine a portion of the challenges to be experienced and how to stay away from them. The globe today could be a great deal more modest spot than it was even 50 years prior. Travel is moderately simple, and the route less expensive than it was once. We tend to go to unfamiliar spots that were once distant to us given cost, troublesome landscape, and political limits. We will, in general, sit in front of the television pictures from the contrary part of the globe radiated to us by satellite, visit online because of the capacity of the net, and text each option on cell phones from wherever the world, for a portion of the worth it was.

The transformation in interchanges has made this potential. Thus, the varieties between the people groups of the world are lessening. We perceive a great deal about each unexpected now in comparison to ever previously. We share ideas and reproduce each of the various designs and technological advancements, yet we never see how our practices and customs vary. Similarly, because you'll knapsack across China, fly to a gathering in Managua, or rest harsh on a Greek occasion seashore, it doesn't mean you see or regard the qualities and uniqueness of individuals and spots you visit. Social variety offers colossal freedoms for getting the hang of concerning and coordinating into each other's societies. All around normally, almost no or no exertion is made to attempt to do as such. Verifiable components are halfway responsible for this, like the 'we tore better than them' mentalities that exist as headaches from the frontier period. In any case, there's no space for this today. Inability to regard the traditions, qualities, and customs of elective nations and people groups is a catastrophe waiting to happen in a multicultural, between subordinate world. The anthropologist, Edward Hall, instituted the saying 'the quiet language' to clarify out-of-mindfulness parts of correspondence. He contended that people of western European plummet live in a 'word world' and generally neglect to understand the meaning of the 'language of conduct.' If we don't, at any rate, attempt to see this language, we can exclusively fault ourselves when things turn out badly. He gives examples in that improper non-verbal conduct, combined with general social harshness, will cause helpless correspondence or perhaps cause it to hinder down out and out.

Take the case in that exchanges among American and Greek officials had arrived at an impasse. The assessment uncovered that the Greeks viewed the American propensity for being candid and frank, showing a shortfall of artfulness that made them hesitant to arrange. When the Americans wished to restrict the length of gatherings and agree on broad standards first, forgetting about the subtleties to be arranged by sub-advisory groups, the Greeks considered this to be an apparatus to pull the fleece over their eyes. The fundamental qualification between the two arranging styles was that the Greeks are generally famous for deciding the subtleties before being completely concerned, paying little attention to the amount of time required. For another situation, an American attaché, new to a Latin nation, attempted to mastermind a gathering with his pastoral inverse assortment. A wide range of messages returned that the time was not all things considered ready for such a social affair. The American continued and was ultimately allowed a preparation. At the point when he showed up, he was approached to go to an external office. The hour of the arrangement traveled every which way. When 1 5 minutes, he requested that the pastor's secretary make positive the priest realized he was pausing. Time passed. Twenty minutes, thirty minutes, 45 minutes. Now, he bounced up and told the secretary he had been 'chilling out long enough which he was 'weary' of this sort of treatment. He had neglected to get a handle on it because a temporary holding up time in that nation was treasure a five-minute holding up time in America. Viable multifaceted correspondence is so fundamental in the cutting-edge world that breakdowns like these need to be ready for the exercises they'll educate us. They moreover fabricate it progressively vital that individuals who live and work in nations other than their own ought to be given training along these lines that they recognize contrasts in neighborhood body language further as the local communicated in language. While a considerable amount of examination has been administered on contrasts in how different people groups throughout the world use body language, it has to focus on the Americans, the Japanese, the Arabs, and a couple of European nations. Extra should be done to incorporate people from various societies given the far greater portability managed by open lines and less expensive travel these days. In an investigation into the usage of eye-to-eye connection, for instance, it's been seen that Greeks inspect each option a ton out in the open spots, regardless of whether in direct correspondence or just perception. They feel furious if elective people don't show equivalent interest in them and feel they are being overlooked. Then again, Swedes have been found to show up at every option less commonly than elective Europeans. However, they give the impression of being for expanded. Bedouins are appallingly dependent on eye-to-eye connection while speaking. They give the impression of being at one another when tuning in and when talking.

How to Change Your Body Language to Help You Be Who You Really Want to Be?
Anyway, they communicate less effectively with somebody whose eyes can't be seen. The Japanese gander at elective individuals next to no and tend to zero in their eyes on the other individual's neck while speaking. Americans and British, then again, tend to be

nearly controlled in their outward appearances, while Italians tend to be considerably more expressive. The Japanese keep a straight face out in the open and utilize grins when welcoming others, all together in business and formal meetings. We will, in general, impart utilizing motions and body pose path extra than we tend to comprehend. Motions, outward appearances, head developments, obviously a wide range of activities including the face, hands, and body, replace words on a few events. Maybe we tend to are moving to the tune of our considerations, contributing what we say with additional significance and weight. Some of the time considerations and sentiments fabricate themselves known while not us proposing them to attempt to 45 along these lines - what we mean by double-crossing our musings. By and large, talk is cheap. How somebody stands will show how they're feeling about something. We tend to call somebody 'tense' when they seem tight and controlling and 'protective' when they fold their arms and hunch their backs. When hello and saying goodbyes, the Japanese bow with lower status bowing people, not exactly those of elevated status. G

remans then again keep a 45 part of upstanding stance than people from Latin nations. Italians and Arabs stand closer to elective people while talking, though Germans stand extra separated. The Japanese utilize formal motions to gather others to them, for example, expanding the arm with palm downwards and vacillating the fingers. To propose that somebody might be a liar, they lick a pointer and stroke an eyebrow. The British are all the more apparent to gesture and look downwards, saying nothing, in any case meaning their uncertainty. Inside the USA, you can flag that all is Well by framing a circle with the thumb and forefinger and fanning out the fingers' remainder anyway. In Japan, a similar signal implies that cash. In France, it implies that 'zero,' in Scandinavia and segments of focal Europe, is viewed as foul, and in some South American nations, it has indecent undertones. In Hindu and Muslim societies, it is standard to utilize the right hand when planning and eating food because the left hand is viewed as messy because of its utilization in important cleanliness. Similarly, pointing the bottoms of your feet towards someone else is viewed as hostile - one thing that globe-running hikers should note. Latins contact each other extra promptly in normal social circumstances than northern Europeans. However, Arab men will often clasp their hands while strolling and talking-one thing that Europeans normally confuse. The Japanese touch every option next to no in broad daylight. However, they have a custom of washing along with no undertone of shamelessness. Western ladies kiss, embrace and spot each other socially, while it is disapproved of for Arab women to be contacted in the smallest degree in broad daylight. As needs are, it ought not to be contacted. In the West, we tend to scratch our heads when we are confused, while in Japan, the indistinguishable activity is deciphered as showing outrage.

Among various non-verbal assortments of correspondence, the manner of speaking is fundamentally essential across societies. Feelings will be checked from how people talk whether the language's communication isn't as expected comprehended. Be that as it may, an expression of caution here: Latin languages are regularly spoken with way more noteworthy accentuation than, say, English and are in the midst of comparatively expressive hand and arm developments. To the more saved northern European, this will work. In elective words, it is up to you, the audience, to perceive and like social contrasts in the methods we impart, not to over-respond to assortments of conduct with which we tend to are new. Similarly, not adjust to our thoughts of adequacy doesn't imply that it isn't right. Americans commonly like a ton of personal space than people in the Mediterranean and Latin American societies and more than men in Muslim societies.

It can be because the house is identified with autonomy and individual rights to protection. In a new report, a Brazilian man filling in as a server in an American eatery found that his propensity for nonchalantly contacting his associates when talking brought about him being dismissed. Befuddled concerning why this was going on, he began to see how Americans cooperate and, in the end, understood that they disdain being moved by what they don't get a handle on. For another situation, an American understudy, who was perusing reasoning at the Sorbonne in Paris, was shocked to see that his Algerian neighbor had a propensity for standing and talking creeps from his face. Not having any desire to appear to be discourteous by stepping back, the understudy conceded that such shut vicinity made him entirely awkward. If an American were to get that closed, he said, he would have responded unexpectedly. It advises us that various societies have unique 'rules of commitment' that break them, even while not knowing, will have negative outcomes. It's uncommon for individuals to have conflicts over close to the home house, presumably because it's exhausting to advise somebody from another culture to backtrack without showing hostility.

A great deal of all the more apparent is that we can point our bodies in such a way as to make a cushion zone between them and us. There is no qualification among us and the rest of the collection of animals in this regard. Creatures don't warmly embrace being moved by outsiders. In this manner, for what reason would it be a good idea for us too? Though it's normally the situation that people grin once they are glad and frown when they are furious, there are loads of courses in that we tend to show non-verbal disappointment with another's practices shrug, for instance. Grins, eye forehead streaks, positioning the zenith, introducing the palm of the right hand in hello - all work with to ease you through the underlying periods of experiences, empowering you at that point to utilize diverse, engaging signals to show what you might want to make reference to or do.

As a rule, a cordial articulation and a sign of interest on the contrary individual will streamline clumsiness, and This is frequently upheld by some attempt to discover catchphrases and expressions from the communicated in language, correspondence is in a flash improve like this, your contrary assortment will very likely meet your 0.5 strategies. Indeed, even we who live in very proper societies, actually like the Japanese, react fright picked words. By examination, in Arab nations, people of senior position and standing tend to be perceived first. Middle Easterners like expressiveness and intermittent showcases of feeling. Gathering vogue business meetings with a few things occurring is ordinary. It isn't uncommon for members to go into shut, individual conversation regardless of the election around them. Africans like to comprehend somebody before getting right serious, and the overall visit toward the beginning of business meetings will seem like time-squandering to outsiders. Time is adaptable, and people who appear to be in a rush are doubted. Delay is a conventional piece of life. Regard is expected to appear to more established individuals. In China, people don't care to be singled out as unmistakable and like to be treated as a group component. Ladies, for the most part, involve significant presents and expect to be treated as equivalents. Long-standing connections are regarded and are valuable, setting aside an effort to decide.

Indeed, even inside the time of email, individual contact is exceptionally esteemed.

Many arranging meetings will typically be required because the Chinese don't wish to surge things. Robert Moran graphically delineates how things can along these lines just turn out badly when you neglect to watch local social varieties in body language. For instance, on the off chance that you need to grab a server's eye at a business lunch in Western nations, a typical strategy is to convey a hand up with the forefinger broadened. In Asia, nonetheless, this is frequently the method you would choose a canine or another creature. In Arab nations, showing the bottoms of your feet is an insult. An Arab could likewise affront somebody by holding their hand before the individual's face. In many components of the planet, shaking the apex proposes that 'No,' anyway in Arab nations and components of Greece, Yugoslavia, Bulgaria, and Turkey, an extra regular route is to throw the top to one aspect, perhaps tapping the tongue too. In] a dish, an individual ran y moves his right hand in reverse and advances to impart a refusal or conflict. In Africa, understanding appears by holding an open palm upstanding and smacking it with a shut clenched hand. Middle Easterners can show arrangement by expanding caught hands with the forefingers pointing towards the other individual. Any individual who embraces global business should do a next to no examination in advance to search out what body language traps should be kept away from. It could fabricate the differentiation between progress and disappointment. In an exceptionally serious world, the financial specialist who neglects to see the value in the force of body language will wrap up paying a high worth. You can improve your body language data as you come by recording your reactions electronically or on a scratchpad. In a way, you may have something to look for counsel from once you filter through the survey segment following each activity.

The Art of Body Language
When you were out with your companions, you, in all likelihood, notice one person who is being overwhelmed by more than one lady. The notification how they're attracted to him, how they tune in to all that he says, and what to look like longingly at him. At that point, you wonder why he was prepared for that. You expect that he makes them thing that makes ladies follow him. You may even reach why you feel that he will have a special necklace that produces young ladies lose their head once they are around him. Sorry to say there is no mysterious recipe, and there's no special necklace. The lone mystery this person has is the authority of the supposed specialty of body language. How you hold yourself, introduce yourself, and act will assemble or break your game. It will make you captivating to ladies or fabricate you show up as though a weakling. When dominating the Art of Body Language, there are three focuses that you need to target. By having some expertise in these significant focuses, you'll have the option to comprehend this craftsmanship better, and the application can be simpler. first, you need to

remember not to exaggerate your activities. The way to radiation sexual appeal is my moving gradually anyway purposely.

Move when you must anyway slither as though you are submerged investigating the globe underneath the surface. Try not to be hesitant to make trying developments as long as it's motivation. Second, you should have the option to order and stand out. You'll have the option to accomplish this by making your quality felt. Use eye to eye connection and slower the standard, worn-out reactions. Be common and go about as though you own the spot. As a great deal of as conceivable is comfortable, recline, unwind, and bless a cheerful disposition and content. Third and last, underline your sexuality. There's nothing amiss with being an individual.

Cause them feel that you're a man by loosening up your lips, shifting your head, and looking at a woman's lips when you're chatting with them. Why is body language thought about craftsmanship? Why is knowing it pivotal to getting higher at deciphering the other sex? These inquiries can be replied by one clear answer: most correspondence is viewed as non-verbal, up to 90%. Those that utilization ninety non-verbal correspondence are savvy at it and have polished it over and over. Assume this technique. Will you utilize non-verbal correspondence to tell an individual how you are feeling and your opinion? Without a doubt, not. In any case, you fall into the 70-eighty.c of people lacking adequate non-verbal abilities.

Those that fall inside the twenty-30p.c of individuals who are fit for non-verbal correspondence consider yourself favored because it is an amazing ability. In any case, this article is intended to help those inside the 70-80p.c find themselves mixed up with the pined for twenty-thirty. Subsequently, what are the keys to progress? As expressed in past articles, everything is awesome anyway, and designs are interminable. The resulting things to appear for aren't unchangeable anyway are a pleasant manual for make from. The first and most significant sort of non-verbal contact is with your eyes. One can't understand how significant the underlying eye to eye connection is because this is the main type of non-verbal contact that one once in a while encounters when adapting to an individual of the other gender. It won't imply that on the off chance that somebody gazes at you that they have an interest which you should gaze back. NO! It is founded on the situational setting.

During a bar, this can be an appropriate presumption because the environment merits it. Nonetheless, when you're at a café getting a charge out of supper with the family, the potential outcomes are is that you have one thing all over. No, essentially joking, there are manners to advise on the off chance somebody is endeavoring to talk with you non-verbally for this situation. In the bar's primary circumstance, the progress from eye language to body language is plentiful quicker. In this way, it is simpler to translate as deliberate non-verbal correspondence. Inside the second situation at the eatery, eye language is the extraordinary kind of non-verbal correspondence because the individual can't utilize their body to talk their sentiments/contemplations. Additionally, on the off chance that you need to test whether they're gazing at you back because you started taking a gander at them. It's basic utilizing your fringe vision, endeavor to find them needing at you. If this occurs time and again, it affirms your underlying contemplations. In case you're trying different things with eye language, general guidelines center around eye language.

Try not to begin joining unpretentious face signals since, in such a case that fouled up, you may look dumb and give the wrong impression. In a very subsequent article, I can get into the body language besides various blends to appear to be out for, or you'll utilize and acknowledge it viable Body language is the most under liked sort of non-verbal correspondence. How might this be? The arrangement is somewhat simple. How might somebody see the value in one thing that they don't comprehend or see how to use? Do you perceive who the biggest guilty party is? Guys! Presently, I will probably ask a ton of messages advising me of how wrong this is regularly. Anyway, it's a long way from this. Before you sign in to your email, think about one inquiry. Does that sex utilize body language the principal and in the entirety of its structures? The arrangement is females. If they use it a great deal of frequently than guys, they'd presumably have a higher eye for body language. A male's virtual device to start body language is his eyes, which are now and then among straight face signals. It is why guys are better at it than females. On the contrary hand, females utilize every one of the types of body language. Not to say that guys don't, anyway it isn't as normal. Young ladies are the 'aces' of body language. The sort of body language used by young ladies relies upon the personality of that singular woman. Bashful and calm ladies once in a while utilize more inconspicuous assortments of body language, which frustrates an individual's capacity to tell whether or not body language is getting utilized. With these assortments of young ladies, the underlying peruses are relentless. In any case, assuming you're ready to get a handle on that woman, over the long run, solace while removing this failure to create discernible body language.

An out-going and fun-loving woman isn't inconspicuous at all when it includes utilizing body language. They use it extra generously and are direct to take note of. They're very timid with their non-verbal correspondence and could raise to slight stroking. Since I referenced it, I can momentarily legitimize the usage of a light touch. It touches conveys messages up to receptors in a man's mind that discharges euphoric synapses. In doing accordingly, the man feels an impression of joy, solace, acknowledgment, and allure across the board, subsequently the euphoric state. The stunt is that you might want to leave them needing more, accordingly leave this slight stroking to a base. Sufficiently not to shape them slobber, but rather not very almost no, they do not feel prodded.

Mastering the Art and Practice of Conscious Body Language

Body language might be an integral asset that may affect the methodology we tend to assume and impact the decisions that we tend to make. When utilized capably, it can impact others and make them think and respond the way you need them to carry on by deliberately projecting your purposeful body developments, outward appearances, and signals first. You may show up and feel extra guaranteed when you utilize good body language. At the point when you move and conduct yourself with certainty and seem to "project" good vibes, you promptly feel extra ready and in charge. Body language correspondence is irresistible. We tend to will, in general, copy each other in discussion. Have you seen how we will generally coordinate with the contrary individual's discourse rate, body developments, motions, and outward appearances? Isn't it eminent that we do this every day when we impart? However, we tend to do consequently without acknowledging it. If you use good body language, the other individual is a great deal of without a doubt to utilize good body language (reflect you), that will thus make the contrary individual feel sure feelings (more joyful, or extra guaranteed in their choices and so on) Caution: The option conjointly remains constant accordingly don't show body language developments, outward appearances or motions which are negative in tone or thought, if your purpose isn't to do hence.

We tend to perceive that utilizing positive body language improves everybody's temperament. Take a gander at how a standup entertainer can utilize the signals, outward appearances, and body developments to make a crowd of people chuckle. Typically, the verbal message is interesting anyway. The body language intensifies the humor and crowd response. Focus on your positive prompts which you project. Construct direct eye to eye connection at whatever point achievable. Comprehend that social contrasts are one of the three keys in body language translation. Grin or loosen up your lips. Abstain from pressing together with your lips or contacting your face more than once. Nobody confides in somebody who contacts their face over and over while talking. Remain with an open stance. Keep your legs and arms free and loose and endeavor to go head-to-head to the perspective, either on a little point to the next individual or right eye to right eye if straightforwardly opposite the other individual. Investigating the left eye of the contrary individual is most agreeable when talking or tuning in. Keep your palms confronted upward and hands loosened up when talking. Significantly, the open palm is uncovered all the more now and again while motioning when talking. It requests to the oblivious brain that you are non-compromising. Keep away from apprehensive or squirming motions like tapping your nails or jingling correction. It signals a significant degree of "inside exchange" or "self-babble" occurring. It will project that you are on edge, anxious, and apprehensive or only wish to move on. Give shut consideration to the body language of the contrary individual as you look after exchange. Watch out for indications of negative body language or signs that the customer is exhausted. It could be having the other individual starting to investigate your shoulder, playing with the zipper on a coat, jingling keys, trimming with random articles, for example, scarves, gloves, and caps. These are showcases of feeling and demeanor. Quietly start to reflect the other individual's body language.

If the customer inclines forward, you should lean forward, showing interest. If they need their arms crossed, fold your arms as well. However, uncover your fingers and assurance they're spread separated. When you're in affinity, start to lead. Test to check whether you'll have the option to lead. For instance, if eating with somebody, go after your water glass. If they also go after theirs and follow your lead, you are currently in affinity! At the point when you might want to infuse a more certain tone into the discussion, gradually move your body language to seem a great deal positive. Uncross your arms and legs, slant your head somewhat when tuning in, and fix your head when talking. Nobody is treated when they talk with a shifted head in the business. (Note: When dating or being a tease, the zenith slant does some incredible things and is very amazing!) It's critical to take note of the ensuing. Do whatever it takes not to change your body language (excessive moving of the body, contacting the face, apprehensive knee developments, figure four) when you begin talking because of this type will flag that you are attempting to take the board of the discussion. If achievable, you're seriously engaging if you'll move to start or during a respite, be the loose instance, and afterward start talking.

So, tune in and deliberately control your body language and notice the responses you get from others. With notice, you may start to see the value because it is so powerful to deliberately utilize your own body to taint the other individual and gain the predefined result you need. To move on from the planet of involvement into the globe of authority infers a readiness to search inside yourself. It implies effectively rehearsing to understand your connection between your body language and hence the feelings, every posture or motion. At some level, we people are largely indistinguishable. Similarly, as pc programming is underlying "stacks," beginning with the machine code level of ones and zeros, we tend to. For our situation, those figurative ones and zeros can address torment/joy, satisfaction/trouble, simplicity, and dis-ease, to call a couple. It would help if you investigated what makes you bright or bleak, making you feel lighter and extra in the stream. At that point, you need to couple that to the language of your body.

At last, you need to apply relating your encounters and sentiments to detect any alliance with comparable body language designs in others. Its technique takes dominating successful delicate abilities. Essentially like scavenging around in a dim and dusty loft, investigating your body language, and like this, the feelings attached to it will seem puzzling, even hazardous. One reason a great many people have, as of not long ago, would, in general, try not to take part during this cycle is that you routinely reveal covered up memories and feelings that you only path back neglected or shrouded where it counts in your tissue. Focusing light on these "issues in your tissues" can be defying and surprisingly excruciating. Be that as it may, staying with this interaction till its total can feel free. It takes stacks of energy to freeze those old feelings set up. By and large, they're like this frozen that muscle will feel like ligament and ligament-like bone. However, for each difficult issue you uncover and adapt to, the energy you were utilizing to remain frozen is freed. You can at present utilize it bountiful all the more proficiently. How may you do extra energy in your life? The other energizing portion of this is that since we are constructed moderately indistinguishable, you may find that others conceal comparative issues in similar physiological spaces of their bodies like you. Consider the possibility that this can be the way to sympathy. We as a whole realize that activity expresses stronger than words. No wonder we will, in general, give like this much significance to body language. There is no reason for clarifying the significance of body language because we tend to secure the force and significance. Right now, the inquiry is will or not it's improved? If yes, how and how much? If you need to upgrade it, it is important to endeavor to comprehend your body language.

You'll soon improve it in like manner. Address your mirror, indeed, follow it before it and endeavor to take a gander at how your body acts in various circumstances, like once you converse with your chief or companions or lady friends. Endeavor to see whether your words are selling great with the body or not. One a ton of issue never attempts to artificial your body language. In the drawn-out, it could land you in soup. Double-dealing can never take you long. Noticing the body language of various people can likewise work with your motivation and amicable arrangement. Watch the renowned people's signal and stance independent of whether they are a celebrity or government official or sports stars and endeavor to decide how they act in certain circumstances, like after they are on sticky wickets. Once, they are glad states of mind. What's more, anon, examine it and afterward take one thing from it, after all in pieces and things.

Anyway, always remember one thing don't copy them completely and take exclusively those motions or stances or developments which fit your demeanor. One more factor, don't mistake quirk for body language. In other words, improve your body language following your demeanor. Improving body language and emulating somebody are two various things. You would potentially have seen that individuals fold their arms or legs while talking. By and large, this signal is related to the safeguard component, which implies that he/she is either cautious or watched, subsequently attempt to stay away from this motion, all things considered while taking. Similarly, raise anybody and be positive everybody can advise you to make an eye-to-eye connection through taking. Indeed, this can be valid. However, make positive you're simply making eye to eye connection and not gazing. The splitting line between eye-to-eye connection and an excess of eye-to-eye connection is thin, making certain of it. Work on your grin and chuckle, since it says a lot about your character; like present yourself cheerfully and afterward be customary don't keep the grinning face all through except if you believe that this is frequently the best technique for you.

Chapter 5: Confident Body Language

Its part will disclose to you how you can conjointly turn out to be so confident that nobody will see on the off chance that you at any point wind up wearing some unacceptable shoes at some unacceptable time regardless of whether they're Crocs. We can likewise investigate the signs for self-assurance and strength and how you'll remember them. These developments, motions, and articulations are normally known as capacity positions because they mirror our inward force. A confident individual persistently embraces a victor make. It is frequently described by the methods you enter and overwhelm a region. The reason comprises a scope of various parts which fabricate clear to others that you are accustomed to winning. You have the stance and the facial demeanor of a champ. Achievement falls into place without a hitch for you, in this manner that you quite recently not might want to think about it. You're open, dynamic, and intriguing, with a loose, anyway, upstanding position. It is like your body seems to refer to: "I feel comfortable here; this can be my region." Winners agreeably enter a space, giving their body masses of house. Their conduct is like a feline, which moves with ease and engages and ceaselessly is by all accounts agreeable in any position. Fearlessness can moreover be shown through loosened-up shoulders and an obvious neck. The shoulders are kept somewhat down, with the chest pushed marginally forward. It represents endeavor, strength, and courage. In ancient occasions, showing your chest was, at that point, an image of self-assurance, showing others that you just had no dread of being injured. People who remain in an upstanding position gaze directly in front of them and are not hesitant to make eye to eye connection.

Lack of Confidence

Through a conference, individuals who push their chest out in this style will acknowledge it simpler to make themselves understood and tuned in to all the more cautiously. Fearlessness is likewise portrayed by an undeniable degree of portability in the jaw when talking. A more extensive opening of the lips all through discourse likewise assists with guaranteeing better elocution. When we will, in general, feel pushed or scared, we tend to commonly agree with the muscles of the jaw, like this that we tend to talk less unmistakably. There are practices you'll have the option to do to loosen up these jaw muscles. One among the most straightforward is to talk your name while you're yawning. You need to attempt to do these activities before your introduction or conversation and not during! Individuals with solid confidence stretch their body out to its full stature. Consequently, they prolong their necks and appearance. Their discussion accomplices straight into consideration. If, for example, you watch a James Bond film, you will see that most of the saints embrace this body position. However, in my skill, it is higher to modify one piece of the Bond cause when you're leading a conference: Try to frame your grin warmth and cordial, instead of cold and dangerous. If your colleague encounters you as somebody warm and agreeable, she will connect this sense with the administrations you wish to offer her. The mix of kind disposition and self-assurance builds your odds of progress.

We referenced that a casual body is a critical component in supporting brilliant associations with others in the past part. It is likewise a sign of self-assurance and control. On the off chance that, for instance, you work in enlisting and are directing a meeting with an applicant, a casual body pose is a savvy intends to see just how confident this competitor truly is. It is particularly useful to tune in to the minutes during the meeting when the applicant tenses and loosens up his body. The degree of pressure that the applicant shows when talking about his past occupation can reveal to you bountiful about his associations with people at his previous manager, how comfortable he felt there, and how much achievement he delighted in. On the off chance that his body is loose, this can indicate that he got masses of positive criticism. The degree of substantial pressure and unwinding will conjointly be utilized to survey how an individual responds to a particular inquiry. If you raise a customer whether she has the necessary spending plan to make a buy and if she unexpectedly becomes tense when she affirms, this could be an indication that she isn't telling the whole truth. Pressure and unwinding of the muscles convey signals that show what segments of the discussion are a ton of intense for your discussion accomplices and that components they feel greater with. A few people are accustomed to working and bantering with, for all time, strained muscles. During this, the body shows that this individual has only requirements for herself.

Importance of Confident Body Language
However, can a strained body assist her with accomplishing her requesting destinations? Or, on the other hand, would it be able to obstruct her? Who might you rather oblige in a client care office, a strained individual, or a casual one? We tend to get the signs of pressure in others at an oblivious level and tend to keep away from tense people because they'll appear to be a possible wellspring of dangers or issues. In qualification, a casual body offers the impression of somebody in administration, somebody who can take care of his undertaking in a contemplated and proper way. On the off chance that you have the propensity for straining your body at work, it very well may be a cunning plan to begin yoga exercises, or swim all the more frequently, or to get yourself a quieting rub. You'll see before long notification that end manages your clients gets simpler. You'll have the option to construct a pyramid alongside your hands by squeezing the tips of your tenderly bent fingers against each other option and shifting them forward at a slight point. The hands will either be stood firm on high or low during the present situation; in different words, at chest level or midsection level. The high variation will regularly be found in people who feel self-assured and prevalent or

in other people who fabricate restricted utilization of body language anyway pick this hand development to underline their vanity. A similar motion is likewise now and again used seeing someone among supervisors and their subordinates. Also, individuals in senior positions frequently show the hand pyramid when disclosing errands to other people or giving a proposal. The indistinguishable is valid for individuals driving conversations, instructors giving talks, and lawmakers giving meetings. The signal promptly recommends somebody who understands what they are talking about and is an expert on the situation.

Therefore, it's the norm with specialists in a few entirely unexpected fields: executives, high sales reps, judges, charge subject matter experts, and so forth. When people are fearless, there is a strong probability that they will frequently construct the pyramid to show that they are sure of themselves and persuaded of the information on what they affirm. If a self-assured individual is tuning in, the pyramid can, as a rule, be held at the lower midsection level. For each situation, the motion is normally a positive sign. Anyway, it's important to see the body language that goes before the motion. If the nonverbal language before the signal was negative, the pyramid's work could be viewed as an affirmation of this negative assessment. A variation of the pyramid is to hold your fingers in a similar bent position. However, instead of squeezing the thoughts along, you keep your hands approximately twenty to thirty centimeters separated.

Because this is frequently generally the position the hands would take if holding a b-ball, the motion is currently commonly alluded to as "holding the ball." once more, it is a signal that oozes fearlessness, yet in an exceptionally subtler and less compromising way than the pyramid. As indicated by a few researchers and customs in different terrains, the thumb could be an image for the inner self. While needing at the position and development of the thumb(s), it's indispensable to comprehend that various understandings are conceivable. By and large, the thumb might be an image of fearlessness. Anyway, it can conjointly be utilized to flag control of a circumstance, cover-up self-importance, or even controlled hostility. In certain societies, bringing the thumb up in an upward position-our natural "alright" motion implies that all is great or working out positively. Turning the thumb during a descending position recommends that the other option: that things don't appear to be fine or not working out positively. Its motion was acquired from the Romans and their gladiatorial challenges. On the off chance that the warrior has battled well, the groups offered him the go-ahead, and he was saved.

However, on the off chance that an overpowered fighter was given the disapproval, it flagged his passing. Its section can reveal to you how you'll also turn out to be hence confident that nobody can see if you at any point notice yourself conveying some unacceptable shoes at some unacceptable time regardless of whether they're

Crocs. We will conjointly inspect the signs for self-assurance and predominance and how you'll remember them. These developments, signals, and articulations are normally called force positions because they mirror our inward force. A self-assured individual perpetually embraces a champ's motivation. It can be described by the way you enter and overwhelm a territory. The posture comprises different parts that make it obvious to others that you're accustomed to winning. You have the stance and, in this manner, the outward appearance of a champ. Achievement works out easily for you, with the goal that you essentially not, at this point, even need to consider the big picture. You are open, energetic, and intriguing, with an open yet upstanding position. Maybe your body hopes to refer to: "I feel comfortable here; this is a regularly my area." Winners agreeably enter space, giving their body heaps of house. Their conduct is like a feline, which moves with smoothness and style and everlastingly appears to be quiet in any position. Self-assurance will likewise be shown through loosened-up shoulders and a noticeable neck.

Confident Body Language - Secrets to Get What You Want!
The shoulders are kept somewhat down, with the chest pushed marginally forward. It represents undertaking, strength, and swagger. In ancient occasions, showing your chest was, at that point, a sign of fearlessness, showing others that you just had no concern of being injured. People who remain in an upstanding position

regularly gaze directly before them and aren't reluctant to make eye-to-eye connections.

During a conference, people who push their chest out in this manner will acknowledge it simpler to make themselves understood and can be tuned in to all the more thoroughly. Fearlessness is furthermore described by an undeniable degree of portability in the jaw when talking. A more extensive hole of the lips during discourse also assists with ensuring better articulation. At the point when we tend to feel focused or scared, we will, in general, commonly will in general agreement the muscles of the jaw, like this that we talk less plainly. There are practices you'll do to loosen up these jaw muscles.

One in everything about best is to talk your name though you're yawning. You wish to do these activities before your introduction or conversation and not all through! Individuals with a solid shallowness stretch their body out to its full stature, so they become 2 or 3 centimeters taller. They stretch their necks and look their discussion accomplices straight in the consideration. If, for example, you watch a James Bond film, you may see that most of the saints receive this body position. In my mastery, yet it is smarter to transform one piece of the Bond present when you're leading a conference: Attempt to make your grin warm and well disposed of, rather than cold and lethal. If your colleague encounters you as somebody warm and well disposed of, she will also connect this sense with the administrations you wish to supply her. The blend of invitingness and self-assurance builds your odds of achievement. In the past section, we tend to reference that a casual body is an essential component in supporting brilliant associations with others. It's conjointly a sign of self-assurance and the board. If, for instance, you're utilized in enlisting and are leading a meeting with an up-and-comer, a casual body stance might be a decent way to deal with see exactly how confident this up-and-comer truly is. It's especially valuable to focus on the minutes all through the meeting when the applicant tenses and loosens up his body. The degree of strain that the competitor shows when talking about his past occupation can reveal to you plentiful in regards to his associations with people at his previous business, how cozy he felt there, and how a ton of progress he delighted in. On the off chance that his body is loose, this will indicate that he got a lot of positive criticism. The degree of substantial strain and unwinding can likewise be utilized to survey how individuals respond to a particular inquiry. On the off chance that you raise a client whether or not she has the obligatory spending plan to shape an obtaining and on the off chance that she out of nowhere becomes tense when she affirms that this could signify that she isn't telling every bit of relevant information.

Strain and unwinding of the muscles convey signals that show that the discussion segments are extra intense for your discussion accomplices and that parts they feel snugger with. A few people are accustomed to working and speaking with forever strained muscles. Along these lines, the body shows that this individual has exclusive standards for herself. Be that as it may, can a strained body truly work with her to understand her requesting goals? Or, on the other hand, will it frustrate her? Who might you rather oblige during a customer administration division, a strained individual, or a casual one? We pick up the signs of pressure in others at an oblivious level.

We will, in general, keep away from tense individuals since they can give off an impression of being an expected wellspring of dangers or issues. Interestingly, a casual body gives the impression of somebody in charge, somebody who will do his assignment in a contemplated and worthy way. If you have the propensity for straining your body at work, it very well may be a savvy thought to begin yoga exercises, or swim a ton now and again, or get yourself an alleviating rub. You may apply before long notification that end manages your clients gets simpler. You'll make a pyramid along with your hands by squeezing the data of your tenderly bent fingers against one another and shifting them forward at a slight point. The hands can either be stood firm on high or low in the present situation; all in all, at chest level or stomach level. The high variation can generally be found in people who feel confident and prevalent or in other people who make confined utilization of body language; however, select this hand development to underline their vanity.

A similar motion is furthermore habitually utilized seeing someone among supervisors and their subordinates. Individuals in senior positions ordinarily show the hand pyramid when disclosing undertakings to other people or offering guidance. The equivalent is valid for people driving conversations, scholastics giving talks, and government officials giving meetings. The signal quickly proposes to somebody whatever they are talking concerning and is expert of valid. Consequently, it is in style with specialists in a wide range of fields: chairmen, high sales reps, judges, charge trained professionals, and so on. When people are fearless, there is a substantial likelihood that they will routinely construct the pyramid to call attention to that they are positive of themselves and persuaded of the information on the thing they are saying. If a confident individual is tuning in, the pyramid can ordinarily be held at the lower stomach level.

For each situation, the motion is, for the most part, a positive sign. However, it's indispensable to see the body language that goes before the motion. If the nonverbal language before the signal was negative, the pyramid's use could be viewed as an affirmation of this negative assessment. A variation of the pyramid is to convey your fingers in the indistinguishable bent position. Instead of squeezing the data together, you keep your hands somewhere in the range of twenty to thirty centimeters separated. Because of this is frequently generally the position the hands would take if holding a b-ball, the signal is presently regularly called "holding the ball." once more, it's a motion that oozes self-assurance anyway an extremely subtler and less compromising way than the pyramid. As indicated by a few researchers and customs on different grounds, the thumb could be an image for the conscience. When taking a gander at the position and development of the thumb(s), it's important to comprehend that various translations are possible. By and large, the thumb could be a picture of self-assurance. Moreover, it will be utilized to flag control of a situation, covered up vanity, or even controlled hostility. In certain societies, bringing the thumb up in an upward position-our recognizable "alright" signal implies that all is great or working out positively. Turning the thumb in a descending position implies that the other option: that things aren't fine or not working out positively. Its signal was acquired from the Romans and their gladiatorial challenges. On the off chance that the combatant has battled well, the groups offered him the go-ahead, and he was saved. Nonetheless, if a squashed warrior was given disapproval, it flagged his demise. We tend to have effectively referenced that the thumb represents the self-image.

It recommends that remaining alongside your hands in your pockets anyway, leaving your thumbs obvious, is another indication of self-assurance, anyway this point with a presumptuous suggestion. There are numerous varieties of this make. For example, if the hands are in the back pockets with the thumbs obvious, the individual being referred to is attempting to shroud predominant propensities. Ladies will utilize their thumbs to broaden predominance. On the off chance that you set your thumbs behind your belt, so your various fingers are set on one or the other part of your sexual organ, this will be an outflow of animosity or sexual interest, contingent upon the specific situation. On elegant occasions, this was (and still is) a make habitually used by cowhand saints in Western films to show the crowd that the said legend was manly.

The make is exceptionally regular for the second when the cowpoke is set up to take out his weapon, sure that his shot will hit home. The posture consolidates two very surprising components: the arms put in a start position and the hands that underscore the body's focal piece. Men embrace this position once they wish to safeguard their domain or exhibit to rivals that they don't feel compromised. Ladies can likewise utilize the indistinguishable position. It has its inceptions in the creature world. Chimps have been seen with their clenched hands on their hips and their thumbs pushed forward during a motion that suggests, "I'm the alpha male, I am the manager here!" It's one of the manners in which that male gorillas search to attract a female mate. Likewise, an individual who turns his body toward a young lady during this posture clarifies that he feels intrigued by her and has sexual expectations.

Winning Ways to Confident Body
In all honesty, it's not your car, your cash, or even your stylish looks that will win you a decent young lady. An

excessive number of men accept this when as a general rule, it's regularly your body language that will draw in a lady to you. Unfortunately, most men are not shown guaranteed body language and the best approach to utilize it. Yet, you'll have the option to learn and build up the guaranteed body language that you might want to draw in a young lady to you. The result is a couple of tips that will work with you to create and utilize your body language to ask the woman you had always wanted. Before you begin to utilize your body language to pull in young ladies, you at first should be intellectually prepared. It's indispensable that you're feeling certain which you're satisfied with yourself likewise.

Disregard any shortcomings that you believe that you may have. Remember, there is no brilliant individual. In case you imagine that contrarily about yourself, it tends to be hard to pull in a young lady, so set aside the negative musings and assume totally and unhesitatingly in regards to yourself. processing might be one among the preeminent indispensable parts of utilizing sure body language. Somebody that is grinning conveys the message that they're certain and content with themselves. On the off chance that you look discouraged, upset, or angry, without a doubt, a woman goes to stay away from you. Anyway, a grin offers a method of welcome to a woman. A grin will fabricate you appear to be congenial besides, and you can show a woman that you are intrigued and prepared to actuate to get a handle on her, just by grinning at her.

Numerous men make the blunder of keeping away from a lady's eyes when conversing with her. Eye to eye connection is one in every one of the first essential kinds of body language. If you can't meet her eyes, it makes you look apprehensive and keep. In any case, a man that shows up somewhere down in her eyes and holds eye to eye connection has all the earmarks of being certain and confident. At the point when you're conversing with a lady, make certain to appear to be straightforwardly in her eyes, and try not to break the consideration contact till she will. Keeping an eye-to-eye connection furthermore causes a lady to feel like you are truly observing her, which can presumably get her to open up to you. It will take thought to make up certain body language; however, utilizing these basic hints can work. Begin rehearsing the accompanying tips and utilizing them, and you will be in a situation to depict a certain picture to women that can be alluring. Collapsing your arms might be a shut position. It implies that you might be concealing something, you're not cozy, you don't wish to talk, or you don't care for what the contrary individual says.

A guaranteed Man is normally cozy and doesn't need to conceal anything. He here and there has his arms by his sides or incompletely in his pockets. Shutting your legs, crossing them, or keeping your feet along would conceivably show weakness. Stand along with your feet more extensively separated. A 4.5-foot ride would be strange. Remain during an agreeable, characteristic methodology. More often than not, you should look the other individual inside the eyes. Try not to gaze at her clumsily; simply get a look to a great extent and keep in touch when you can. Never gaze at the base when conversing with somebody by the same token. You're not a youngster who got unfortunate evaluations in school and is reluctant to converse with daddy. Turn away aside, however, never down. Certainty should be transmitted from your look. Stand erect, and don't a though your back. Also, since I speculate nobody pushed a post-up your butt, don't stand immovably in a hardened methodology. You can bear losing while not curving your back, correct? Right. It's eternity a tricky arrangement to grin. It hinders individuals. It's logically demonstrated that grinning can't exclusively give positive sentiments to the grin, however to the smiler moreover.

Indeed, that is you. So don't be hesitant to attempt to do it. It would help if you did not consistently have a major smile all over. Anyway, when conversing with ladies or moving toward a young lady, make sure to grin a ton. It establishes a keen connection and even assists her with unwinding while at the same time conversing with you. She won't be just about as apprehensive as she would be on the off chance that you drew nearer with an authentic look all over. Along these lines, recollect what I say and drop the macho thing. A guaranteed individual is normally in an extremely loose and agreeable state. He tries not to take fast actions. He doesn't play along with his fingers or shakes his legs anxiously. Each move you make and each muscle you move should be the aftereffect of a conscious choice and not brought about by uneasiness. Walk gradually, anyway, nonchalantly. Try not to walk like a robot, please. Be without a care in the world. You're not during a rush. You don't need to run. You're not being pursued. Move at your speed. Furthermore, don't be hesitant about needing up some space as you progress. You don't have to guide along with your hands unfurl vi feet separated, anyway show that you'll fill the region around you.

CONCLUSION

Thank you so much for purchasing this book.

I hope you enjoyed the book. Body language is as significant in correspondence as talking, tuning in, perusing, and composing. It could be contended that it's a ton of fundamental gave that yet 10% of what we will, in general, impart to others is looking like words. It is exclusively moderately late that the spotlight has focused on the non-verbal pieces of language and conduct. Because of spearheading work across a few controls - from zoology to paralinguistics - we will, in general, perceive more about human correspondence these days than whenever in our set of experiences. Examination in chronemics, haptics, kinesics, proxemics, and neurolinguistic programming has made us fully aware of the current dynamic universe of signs and signals, where hints, thought processes, aims, sentiments, and decisions are communicated through refined motions, signs, and significant developments. We tend to utilize the body's language to pass on implicit contemplations, and we take as a correct that others will see our implications. Quite a bit of this occurs at an inner mind level.

We may not recollect that our outward appearances, hand developments, winks, squints, gestures, and moans are conveying messages of insistence, analysis, interest, or hatred. The intention is that language doesn't need to be looking like words for importance to be gotten a handle on by others. The methods you utilize your body resemble 'accentuation.' Without it, stress is lost. Ideally, this book has given you the information you need to turn into a ton of achieved communicators. By utilizing what you have figured out how to build your self-assurance and improve your exhibition, you'll start to procure the benefits in your connections, at work, and in your ordinary experiences with others.

Cheers!

Lightning Source UK Ltd.
Milton Keynes UK
UKHW020705040521
383105UK00011B/575